JOHN CABOT
& THE VOYAGE OF THE MATTHEW
LIVING HISTORY IN COLOUR

BRIAN CUTHBERTSON

FORMAC PUBLISHING COMPANY LIMITED
HALIFAX

Formac Publishing Company Limited acknowledges the support
of the Department of Canadian Heritage and the Nova Scotia
Department of Education and Culture in the development of
writing and publishing in Canada. We acknowledge the support
of the Canada Council for the Arts for our publishing program.

Formac Publishing Company Limited
5502 Atlantic Street
Halifax, Nova Scotia
B3H 1G4
Printed and bound in Canada.

Canadian Cataloguing in Publication Data

CUTHBERTSON, Brian, 1936 -

    John Cabot and the Voyage of the Matthew.

    Includes bibliographical references
    ISBN 0-88780-416-0

1. Cabot, John, d. 1498?   2. Matthew (Ship)
3. America — Discovery and exploration — British.
I. Title

FC301.C3C87 1997970.01'7'092
C97-950139-3   E129.C1C87 1997

For photo credits, see page 72

Distributed in the United States by
Seven Hills Book Distributors
49 Central Avenue, Cincinnati, Ohio 45202

CONTENTS

PREFACE

Five hundred years ago, on 24 June 1497 John Cabot, sailing out of Bristol, England in the *Matthew*, made a North American landfall somewhere between Cape Sable in southwestern Nova Scotia and the Strait of Belle Isle in northern Newfoundland. When on that June 24th Cabot raised the royal standard of King Henry VII, laying claim to the land for England, he believed he had reached northern Asia and the Land of the Great Khan, with its untold riches in spices, gold, and silks. As succeeding explorers were to discover, neither Christopher Columbus in 1492 nor Cabot in 1497 had reached Asia, but a new world. Their voyages initiated an era of expansion for Europeans, the consequences of which continue to dominate world history. For aboriginal inhabitants, these voyages meant the seizure of their lands and still threaten their cultural destruction.

One of the extraordinary ironies of Cabot's story is that the seemingly endless controversy over his 1497 landfall has so dominated debate that the man and his achievements seem often to have been lost. This book on Cabot, there-fore, concentrates on the man, his understanding of world geography, and how he came to sail out of Bristol and west across the Ocean Sea in May 1497. As far as his landfall is concerned, I lay out the arguments for either a Cape Breton or a Newfoundland site. I believe, however, the debate unresolvable, given the records we have.

By writing this book on John Cabot, I hope to make a literary contribution to the 500th anniversary celebra-tions. At the centre of these festivities, of course, has been the building in Bristol of a replica of the *Matthew*. The *Matthew* is now well on her way across the Atlantic and set to arrive on 24 June at Bonavista, the traditional site for Newfoundlanders of Cabot's landfall. There the *Matthew* will be welcomed in full royal pageantry by Queen Elizabeth and Prince Philip.

After Bonavista, the *Matthew* will sail around Newfoundland to visit various communities whose names are redolent of the earliest European voyaging to

Above: The Matthew, *heading down the Avon for her sea trials*
Opposite: The Matthew, *1995*

North America by English, French, Basque, and Portuguese explorers and fishermen — Grates Cove, Harbour Grace, St. John's, Placentia Bay, Grand Bank, Harbour Breton, Burgeo, Port aux Basques, Red Bay, St. Anthony, La Scie, Twillingate, and Trinity. Then the *Matthew* will cross the Cabot Strait, first to Neil's Harbour near Cape North at the top of Cape Breton Island and the place that many believe was Cabot's first sight of land, and on to Sydney, Halifax, Shelburne, and Yarmouth. From there the *Matthew* will sail down the American coast to visit various ports.

In writing this biography, I have followed a chronological approach, with each chapter presenting a different phase of Cabot's life. Cabot is believed to have been born around 1450 in Genoa, but his family left for Venice when he was a youth to seek better opportunities in the lucrative eastern spice trade. In Venice, Cabot became a citizen, which allowed him to participate in the spice trade. He went to Mecca at the risk of his life to find where the spices came from. He was in Valencia, Spain in 1492 when Christopher Columbus passed through on his way to tell King Ferdinand and Queen Isabella he had reached the East. Among those who didn't believe Columbus had reached Asia, but rather some other land or islands, was John Cabot, who came to believe that by sailing on a more northern latitude he himself could reach Asia and the Land of Great Khan. How he convinced, first the merchants and seamen of Bristol, and then King Henry VII, of the practicality of his idea is an important part of the Cabot story and essential to an understanding of his epic 1497 voyage. I have tried to provide readers with a balanced appraisal of contending schools of opinion on where Cabot went. No aspect of his voyaging, however, has been more analysed with so little success as the cartographical evidence. In Chapter 9, I summarize contemporary opinion on two of

the most enigmatic maps, la Cosa's of 1500 and Sebastian Cabot's of 1544. The controversy over where Cabot first sighted land, his *prima terra vista*, has a history all its own. In the concluding chapter, I trace the history of the debate over the centuries to the present time: needless to say, determining his landfall continues to be as elusive as ever and has become the chief mainstay to the mystique that has grown up around the man and his voyages.

In the last chapter, I also discuss how the 400th anniversary of Cabot's 1497 voyage was commemorated in Halifax, St. John's, and Bristol. A crucial difference between 1897 and the yearlong festivities arranged for the 500th anniversary is that no permanent legacy seems to be planned at this time. In 1897, both St. John's and Bristol got their Cabot Towers. In 1997, the best hope for such a permanent legacy bringing long-term community benefit is a proposed John Cabot Heritage Centre at Cape North on Cape Breton's Cabot Trail. If this book helps to bring this centre to reality, it will for me be worth all the effort that has gone into its research and writing.

No book is entirely an author's own effort. I wish especially to acknowledge the financial aid of the John Cabot Meeting Society of Cape North, without which this book would never have been published. The challenge of obtaining, from both sides of the Atlantic, the book's visual material was a new and interesting experience and could not have been accomplished without the helpful assistance of the staff at Formac Publishing. This is my ninth book, and I have learned the critical importance of having a good editor. Scott Milsom has performed this task for me admirably, though I, of course, accept full responsibility for any errors or lapses in clarity.

— *2 June 1997, Brian Cuthbertson*

The publisher and author wish to recognize the valuable contribution of the John Cabot Meeting Society (JCMS) in financing the costs of visual research for this book. The JCMS is the non-profit organization formed in February 1996, to plan and implement "Reflections/The Cabot Meeting '97," the year-long commemoration of the historic 1497 voyage of John Cabot and the beginning of North American and European relations.

Opposite: The Matthew *passes St. Michaels Mount, Cornwall*

Above left: Newfoundland ten-cent stamp, 1897

Left: A recent enactment of John Cabot's landing at Cape North overlooking Aspy Bay, Cape Breton

*This 16th-century view of Genoa with
numerous ships in the harbour, by
Christoforo Grassi, shows the city's
dependence on maritime commerce*

GENOA

I have seen the map made by the discoverer [John Cabot] who is another Genoese like Columbus

— Pedro de Ayala to King Ferdinand and Queen Isabella, 25 July 1498

*T*his ambassadorial despatch on John Cabot's 1497 voyage of discovery west across the Atlantic provides us with the chief reliable evidence of Cabot's Genoese origins. We do not know Cabot's date of birth, though a most likely date is around 1450 or earlier. That his birth went unrecorded was not surprising: births were seldom recorded anywhere in Europe and few of Cabot's contemporaries knew their exact age. One in four children died within their first year, half would be dead by their twentieth. Famine, plague, disease, and violence on a massive scale all contributed to keep life expectancy to between 30 and 35 years. A century before Cabot's birth, the Black Death had swept through first Italy and then the whole of Europe. It and succeeding epidemics had so devastated Genoa by 1400 that its population of 40,000 was still only two-thirds what it had been a century before.

The Black Death came to Italy before the rest of Europe because Genoa and Venice controlled sea-borne trade with the East, where the plague originated. Both these city-states grew rich and powerful from trade. During the Crusades to capture the Holy Land from the infidel Muslims, Genoa and Venice prospered greatly from transporting and supplying the Christian armies. The Crusades gave medieval Europe a taste for luxury and the exotic, creating a seemingly insatiable demand for spices, silk, slaves, porcelain, ivory, gems, and eastern foods. Genoese and Venetian merchants purchased these goods from Muslim merchants who themselves had imported them over land and sea routes that reached from Japan and China, through the Indonesian archipelago, and around India to the eastern Mediterranean and Black Sea ports, a distance of 15,000 kilometres. Large galley fleets then transported these goods throughout the Mediterranean and as far as Flanders and England, where they were sold at great profit. To protect and increase this trade, both Genoa and Venice established fortified colonies and merchant enclaves in the eastern Mediterranean. They also fought each other in a series of naval wars that by 1400 gave the Venetians maritime dominance.

Other than that there were Cabotos (the name means "coaster," as in coastal shipping) in Genoa, we know very little of John's family. In Genoa, more than in any of the other Italian city states, the *albergo*, or clan, dominated political, social, and commercial life. A clan consisted of an association of families whose members had long-standing ties of interdependence and obligation. Clan membership provided protection and assistance in times of need. Such was their importance that John Cabot's father, Egidius, could only have pursued his mercantile activities as a clan member. Family connections provided the glue that bound together expatriate confraternities of Genoese merchants who established themselves in the major trading ports from the eastern Mediterranean, through the Strait of Gibraltar, to Bristol and London.

Both John Cabot and Christopher Columbus (also Genoese and born in 1451, and therefore about the same age as Cabot) would later turn for assistance to these clannish commercial communities.

Although Columbus came from a weaver's family, he went to sea at a very early age, likely through family connections with a merchant-clan. Cabot, himself the son of a merchant, almost certainly did the same. Childhood, as we understand it today, did not exist in medieval Europe: parents dressed their children as adults and put them to work as early as possible. In common with his contemporaries, Cabot would have learned the mariner's trade by observation and experience. By the mid-1400s, the Genoese had largely shifted from galleys to bulk-cargo sailing ships, and Cabot likely sailed in a carrack, or in a smaller version of this type of broad-hulled sailing vessel.

We know Columbus received no formal education and there is no reason to believe Cabot did so either. Both,

however, came of age as Gutenberg's invention of moveable type was making printed books available on such a scale that by 1500 perhaps six million copies had been produced. What we know of Cabot suggests that he read less widely than Columbus. As nothing he may have written has survived, it's a fair assumption that he wrote little, in contrast to Columbus, who wrote much for his day and annotated his readings. Practical experience in navigation and maritime commerce, along with a modicum of self-education, sufficed for the youthful Cabot to make his way as a merchant-mariner.

Throughout much of Genoa's history, continual civic discord plagued the city. Innumerable revolutions by feuding factions generated such instability that it was remarkable Genoa sustained its rivalry with Venice as long as it did. A period of particularly violent turbulence began in the 1430s, when civil war broke out and continued on and off for four years. Genoa suffered a major loss when in 1453 the Ottoman Turks seized Pera, a prized merchant colony in Constantinople. Elsewhere in the Levant, Genoese merchants found it increasing difficult to compete with the Venetians, who were much better organized and gained advantageous privileges from Muslim rulers at Damascus and Alexandria. Spice prices on the European market also fell drastically from the high levels of the 1420s. As a result, Genoese merchants began withdrawing from the spice trade to invest in the expanding economies of Spain and Portugal. It may have been because of the city's withdrawal from the spice trade, or perhaps it was just the prevailing anarchy, but sometime in the 1450s Egidius Caboto and his family of least two sons, Zuan (John) and Piero (Lewis) left Genoa for Venice.

Genoese Fleet Moored in the Port of Genoa, *by Giorgio Vigne, 1618*

Chapter Two

VENICE

He [John Cabot] says that on previous occasions he has been to Mecca, whither spices are borne by caravans from distant countries... He therefore reasons that these things [spices] come from places far away from them, and so on from one to the other, always assuming that the earth is round, it follows as a matter of course that the last of all must take in the north towards the west

— Raimondo de Raimondi de Soncino to the Duke of Milan, 18 December 1497

When the Cabot family arrived in Venice, the city was at its zenith as the foremost Meditrranean naval and commercial power and the strongest state in Italy. After one visit, a French ambassador wrote that Venice was the "most triumphant city I have ever seen, does most honour to all ambassadors and strangers, governs itself with

Procession in Piazza San Marco, by Gentile Bellini, 1496. The Basilica of San Marco is in the background. In the foreground are the Doge and Venetian Magistrates

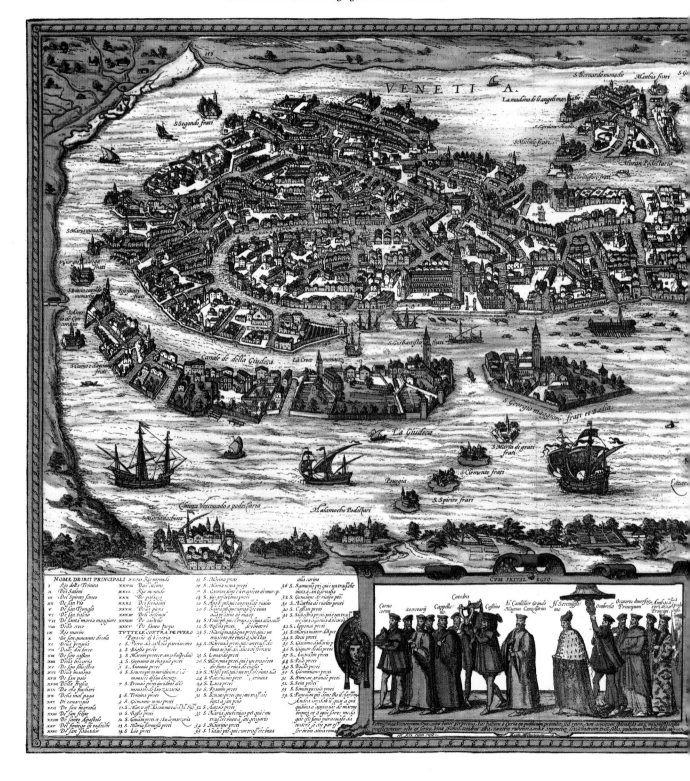

ila preti	*79 La madona de l'arfenale*
preti	*80 La ca de dio*
m don e il trag°di l'uafofma	*81 S spulcro monache*
ti	*82 La piera*
ri qui e il trag°che bura alla giudoca	*83 La celestia monache*
qui e vn triu°che bura a S.ftephano	*84 S Francifco della migna frati*
reti	*85 S Giouan de furlani priorado*
preti	*87 S Giorgio di greci preti greci*
preti	*88 S Lorenzo monache*
uador frati qui e la fcola grando	*89 S Zacharia monache*
rtofomio piron: fi S°todoro	*90 S Giouan polo frati*
Gregorio preti	*171 Scuola grande de fan marco*
Marciltano preti	*172 S Gio laronin monache*
ftina monache	*91 L fofpdai di fan gioanne polo*
ucia monache	*92 Madona di miracoli monache*
fe monache	*93 I crofachieri frati*
na	*94 S Caronina monache*
CHIESE	*95 S Maria della valuerde fena la*
monache	*mifcricordia fcuola grade et priorado*
no monache	*96 S Maria dell'orti frati*
onache	*97 S Aluje monache*
frati	*98 I forni frati*
o fofpedale	*99 S Hicronimo monache*
monache	*100 S Iob frati*
rifto fofpedale	*102 Il corpus domini monache*
onio frati	

DELLE COSE PIV NOTABILI
131 Arfenale nuouo
132 Arfenale vecchio
133 Porta dell'arfenale
134 Il fignor bartfolamio cogtione
135 La boca della marzaria fcoto il relois
136 Le due colonne doue fi fa iußiria
137 Il campali di fan marco
138 La porcuraria noua di fan marco
139 La cea
140 La peffaria di fan marco
141 Il fontego di tedefchi
142 Li magazini dni fale
143 La doana da mare
144 Ghero doue ftano li hebrei
145 Le cafe da ca moro
146 Berfaglio doue fifer cinm fibobar dieri
147 Pefaria di rialto
148 Il ponte da caftello e e di legno
149 Il ponte di bareri fufa marzaria
150 Il ponte di rialto e di legno co molte
boeghe fopra dall'vna et l'altra
parte ee fi apre due parte
151 Il ponte di canaregio e di legno
152 Il ponte dla pagla
153 Campalco

the greatest wisdom..." With a population of 100,000, it ranked after only Naples as the largest city in Italy and was among the most populated in Europe. Its republican constitution — with a balanced division of powers among a hierarchy of councils composed of hereditary nobles, and at its apex the Doge, elected for life — gave Venice an envious domestic stability and an impartial judicial system that markedly distinguished it from the rest of Europe.

In 828 A.D., Venetian merchants smuggled relics of Mark the Evangelist out of Alexandria in Egypt and brought them to Venice. Saint Mark became the city's patron saint and his representation as a winged lion came to symbolize Venetian maritime supremacy. The city's most famous building was St. Mark's Basilica, where the adjoining square served as a public concourse for great state occasions. Along the Grand Canal were the palaces of the nobility and such public buildings as the Ducal Palace, where the Doge resided. Also on the Grand Canal was the Rialto, where merchants did their business and ships unloaded their cargoes, for Venice's wealth came from a maritime empire created over four centuries of war and commerce.

Fifteenth-century Venice was unlike any other city of its day. It had been built up over the centuries by connecting a maze of islands within lagoons to a series of canals, bridges, and timber pilings until a great metropolis had been created. The lagoons and surrounding marshlands protected Venice from landward attack, obviating the need for city walls. As long as Venice could defeat her enemies at sea, she did not fear direct attack. Only once did Venetians believe their city's very existence threatened. During the fourth war with Genoa in 1378-79, Genoa's allies established a blockade on the landward side while the Genoese, having defeated a Venetian fleet,

Map of Venice, 1578

Above: The Miracle of the Holy Cross, *by Vittore Carpaccio, late 15th century. The bridge is the Ponte di Rialto where John Cabot would have spent much time as a merchant-mariner making arrangements for going to Alexandria with the Great Galley fleet*

Opposite top: Plan of Venice by Odoardo Fialetti, 16th-17th century

Opposite bottom: Map and plan of Venice showing ships in the canals and the lagoon, by G. B. Arzenti, late 16th or early 17th century

mounted a land- and sea-blockade on the seaward approaches. The city was on the point of surrendering from starvation when the timely arrival of another fleet, which had been raiding Genoese commerce, saved it by blockading in turn the Genoese attackers and forcing their surrender. Genoa never fully recovered from this defeat at the very sea gates of her greatest enemy and commercial rival.

The foundation of Venetian naval strength and wealth lay in her great galleys built by the state-run Arsenal, the largest industrial complex in Europe. By the time the Cabot family arrived, the Arsenal had the capability to construct and outfit simultaneously over 80 galleys. These, with 150 oarsmen each and using lateen sails, could reach up to seven knots for short periods and were highly maneuverable in battle and for entering harbours. The Venetians divided their merchant galleys into seven great convoys that sailed regularly each year throughout the Mediterranean and as far as Flanders and England.

Of these fleets, the most important was the Galley of Alexandria, which brought back each winter 2,500 tons of spices. At the Rialto, Venetian merchants sold the spice cargoes to foreign merchants or trans-shipped them on the Flanders Galley fleet.

Continual wars and outbreaks of plague made for such high death rates that Venice could only renew itself by attracting immigrants. But by no means did all immigrants become naturalized, nor did all native-born Venetians obtain citizen rank. Citizens formed a middle class whose members held themselves above any mechanical employment. From this class the state recruited its officials. Other citizens engaged in commerce and held the same rights to trade as nobles. Venice closely controlled foreign merchant activity, and terms of citizenship referred directly to trading rights.

Around 1472 John Cabot gained Venetian citizenship. Venetian law required a well-attested residency of fifteen years as a law-abiding taxpayer before citizenship could be granted, so Cabot must have been in Venice by 1457. In Cabot's Italy, a man could participate in civil life at fourteen years of age, and the church assumed at this age a knowledge of what constituted mortal sin. At fifteen, young men could be required to pay taxes and for

military service. Although his citizenship's "terms of privilege" provided him with all "the liberties, rights and immunities that the other Venetians, our citizens, have and enjoy within and without," he could not himself trade nor carry on trade through others by sea until he had given security to the government. Without that right to trade, citizenship would not have benefitted Cabot greatly. Only when he had the financial resources to provide the security demanded would he have sought citizenship: it is doubtful he could have put up such

security until he was twenty or older.

Venetian men did not marry until their thirties, though women were usually in their twenties when they wed. The time needed to create the financial means to establish a household and a division of family property on a son's marriage both worked to delay marriage. There was also a sexual imbalance, with men considerably outnumbering women, thus making the finding of a suitable wife more difficult. Cabot seems to have married about 1480, when, if we accept a birth date of 1450, he

Healing of Man Possessed by the
Devil, *by Vittore Carpaccio, showing
Grand Canal and Rialto Bridge in
Venice, late 15th century*

16

was 30 years old. We know his wife's name was Mattea
and that by 1484 they had two or more sons. From a
series of surviving property transactions in 1483 and
1484, it appears John Cabot did well as a merchant and
became moderately well off: in one case he sold property
for 1,600 ducats. Such a sum was substantial, given the
700-ducat average annual income of a Venetian noble, or

the 28 ducats of a galley oarsman.

For the low-volume, but extraordinarily lucrative trade in spices and silks, Venetian merchants used the great merchant galleys for which the city was famous. Each year the Senate auctioned off these state-owned galleys to merchant partnerships. It also appointed the overall flotilla commander and the captain of each galley, while the Doge and chief magistrates chose by ballot the chief navigator, or *armiraio*, for the voyage, though each galley had its own navigator as well. Because the chief navigator came from among the most skilled seamen in the city and held the highest paid non-noble

position in a galley flotilla, his prestige was great. Chief navigators, such as Andrea Bianco, a renowned map maker, kept extensive sailing records, and by Cabot's day Venetian seamen had accumulated an unrivaled knowl-

A portolan of the Italian Peninsula showing the geographical relationship of Genoa and Venice

way of the Arabs. Although they portrayed only shore-lines and made no allowance for the earth's curvature, a navigator could roughly plot his bearing from port of departure to destination on a *portolan*. John Cabot would have learned how to navigate using compass and charts, and he would also have been instructed in the use of tables that allowed a navigator, when he had lost his compass direction, to recover his true course.

Venetian "Great Galleys" could carry 250 to 300 tons of cargo. As passengers, they carried merchants and government officials. The Alexandria Galley, usually of five to seven vessels, left to purchase spices in the early autumn, carrying as much as 100,000 ducats in gold and silver. By Christmas, the fleet returned to Venice with its valuable cargoes. We do not know how often Cabot sailed with the great Alexandria Galley fleet or in what capacity. He might have gone as a lower-ranking officer, but he probably went as a merchant representing a partnership. Nonetheless, he had the opportunity to learn much about navigation and hone his mariner's skills under the master navigators of the day.

Cabot claimed that on a number of occasions he went to Mecca, Islam's holiest city, to discover, if he could, where the spices came from. The Arab rulers of Egypt, called Mamelukes, whose empire extended over Syria and Palestine, maintained absolute control over the spice trade with Europeans. On their long journey of six months to two years from the Far East, the spices came by sea to Mecca's port of Jedda on the Red Sea. There, Arab merchants organized camel caravans and vessels to carry the spices to Alexandria. The Mameluke rulers had allowed the Venetians and others to establish warehouses at Alexandria within strictly confined compounds: those of the Venetians were reputed to be the finest buildings in the city. They forbade Christians to leave their compounds during the hours of prayer on the Muslim holy day of Friday and all Christians were locked in their compounds each night. Aside from protecting the undefiled from associating with infidels, the Mameluke rulers, whose rapacious greed became legendary, took whatever actions, however brutal, that were necessary to ensure the rich spice trade remained firmly in their hands.

How Cabot got from Alexandria to Mecca is unknown.

edge of the Mediterranean and for navigating to Flanders. These sailing records took the form of navigation charts, called *portolans*, and were largely the production of Venetian and Genoese map makers. *Portolans* were based on mariners' direct observation and the use of the compass, knowledge of which had come to Europe from China in the twelfth century by

An Arab merchant and his nephew arriving in Mecca

If captured, as a Christian he faced slavery and forced conversion at best, and a most cruel death at worst. He could have travelled — presumably in some disguise unless he had somehow obtained by bribery or other means Mameluke permission — with a caravan returning to Mecca down the eastern coast of the Red Sea. Most likely, however, he descended the Nile to its first cataract, then crossed by caravan to the Red Sea port of Koddeir, and from there went by sea to Jedda. Arab merchants favoured the latter route because the long land journey up the coast lay so open to attack by marauding tribesmen, even though Mameluke rulers provided soldiers to protect camel caravans and issued safe-conduct passes to merchants.

It was the rich profits to be made in the spice trade that drove men such as Cabot to seek to by-pass the Mamelukes and trade directly with the Spice Islands. Europeans' knowledge of the far east was, however, hazy indeed. Much of what they knew came from *The Travels of Marco Polo,*

Map of Alexandria, from the 16th century

or, as it was originally titled, *Description of the World*. It first began circulating in 1301 in numerous manuscript copies before being printed during the next century and having a remarkably wide readership throughout Europe.

As frightful, cruel, and devastating as were the thirteenth-century Mongol conquests under the much-feared Ghengis Khan and his near invincible hordes of horsemen-bowmen, from them came a *Pax Mongolica* from 1260 to 1368. This Mongol-imposed peace over its vast empire — which stretched from the outer reaches of China, where the Great Khan ruled, through central Asia to Persia and around the Black Sea and deep into southern Europe — allowed Europeans to travel eastwards in relative security. Under Mongol rule commerce prospered. European merchants, diplomatic envoys, and Christian missionaries found the khans open to foreign contacts, ideas, and, above all, trade.

Probably the first Europeans to reach China were the Venetian merchant brothers Nicolo and Maffeo Polo. After travelling from Constantinople into the Crimea on a trading venture that proved highly lucrative, they found their return blocked by a war between two rival khans. The intrepid brothers decided to push further east to Bukhara, where they joined a foreign embassy making its way to the Great Khan, Kublai. Finally, in 1261, they reached China, where Kublai made them welcome, and they remained there until 1269. They then returned home, where they told of the immense wealth and splendour of the Mongol court and its desire for trade. Three years later, accompanied by Nicolo's son, Marco, the brothers set off again on a trading mission to China. Marco Polo's *Travels* tells of their three-year journey overland along the Silk Road to fabled Cathay, their years in the Great Khan's service, and their return to Venice in 1295 by the South China Sea and Indian Ocean. Marco did not write the *Travels*. Rusticiano, a professional writer of romances of the day, wrote them

down from what Marco told him while both he and Marco were in a Genoese prison, Marco having been captured during one of the numerous sea battles between Genoa and Venice.

Marco's *Travels* are filled with such fantastic imagery that even in his day there were disbelievers. (His use of widely exaggerated numbers earned him early the humerous epithet of *Marco Millioni*.) But what most fascinated medieval readers were his vivid descriptions of the splendour of Kublai Khan's palaces, the greatness of his empire, and the wealth in gold and precious stones to be found in the marvelous cities he visited. Always the merchant, Marco reported extensively on the expansive trading network throughout China, to the Spice Islands (Java and Sumatra) and around to India. He told of ports filled with vessels capable of carrying far larger cargoes than European ships, and of how the use of paper money, completely unknown to Europeans, underpinned this vast trading network. Thirteenth-century Europeans could only marvel at such colourful accounts as that of Cipangu (Japan) which Marco never visited, but only recounted what he had heard of its immeasurable wealth — of gold in so great abundance that his readers:

> could take it for a fact that [the ruler] has a very large palace entirely roofed with fine gold... And the value of it is almost beyond computation. Moreover all the chambers, of which there are many, are likewise paved with fine gold to a depth of more than two fingers' breadth. And the halls and the windows and every other part of the palace is of such incalculable richness that any attempt to estimate its value would pass the bounds of the marvelous... They have pearls in abundance, red in colour, very beautiful, large and round. They are worth as much as the white ones, and indeed more... They also have many other precious stones in abundance. It is a very rich island, so that no one could count its riches.

Marco placed Cipangu some 1,500 miles east of China. Of all the places he recounted in his *Travels*, Cipangu was to figure most prominently in the minds of

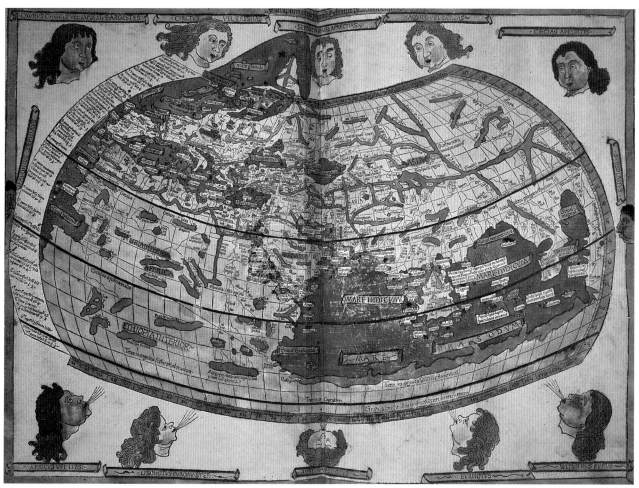

Christopher Columbus and John Cabot when each in turn set out to sail west and reach fabled Cathay.

Although Marco's *Travels* provided both Columbus and Cabot with much of their knowledge of the East, Cabot would also have heard or read about the travels of merchants closer to his own time. Among the most extraordinary were those of the Venetian merchant Nicolò Conti. Conti's intrepidity took him on a sea voyage from the Persian Gulf to India, and on to the Spice Islands, back across to the Red Sea and Jedda before reaching Alexandria, and then home to Venice: in all, he was away for 25 years, from 1419 to 1444. He found it wise at one point to renounce his Christianity and become a Muslim. Once safely back in Italy, he sought forgiveness from the pope for his forced apostasy, who as penance ordered him to relate his journeys to Poggia Bracciolini, the papal secretary.

None of Ptolemy's maps has survived, but medieval Europeans created reconstructions from his Geographia, *such as this one of the 15th century. Note the use of longitude and latitude. The exhaling heads represent winds*

Conti provided Europeans with the most detailed knowledge they would have of India and the Spice Islands until Vasco da Gama rounded the Cape of Good Hope and reached India in 1498. Although Conti mentioned Cathay, he never went there. He seems to have relied entirely on Marco Polo's *Travels* in his description of Cathay, even reporting that the ruler was the Great Khan, though a native Chinese dynasty, the Mings, had overthrown Mongol rule some 60 years previously. Not until the first decade of the sixteenth century were Europeans to know of the Mongol Empire's demise. For Cabot, Conti's account of Cathay would have confirmed what he read in Marco's *Travels*.

Cabot was by no means alone in going from Alexandria to Mecca. Other Genoese and Venetian merchants also made their way there, while the most adventurous continued across the Indian Ocean on Arab trading vessels to the Spice Islands. When, for example, the Genoese merchant, Girolamo di San Stefano, reached Sumatra in 1494, he found an Italian-speaking official who fortuitously intervened to save San Stefano's goods from confiscation. On behalf of King Afonso V of Portugal, Pedro de Covilhão, in his search for a new route to the Spice Islands in the 1480s, claimed to have travelled up and down the Red Sea four times and visited Mecca in disguise. None of these dauntless travellers, however, seem to have made their way to China.

Cabot may not have read Bracciolini's version of Conti's journeys, which he wrote in Latin and manuscript copies of which early became rare. But because Conti returned to Venice and presumably died there only twenty years or so before Cabot received Venetian citizenship, his journeys must have been common knowledge on the Rialto. Conti's reports certainly had a

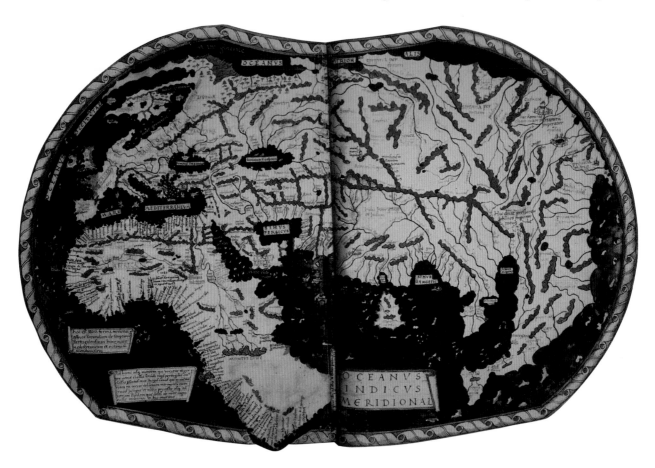

major influence on Venetian and Genoese map makers' portrayals of the East. Venetian map makers maintained workshops that were leading centres for integrating the practical knowledge gained by seamen with the new geographical learning derived from both classical sources and increased scholarly speculation. Cabot probably worked for a time in one of these workshops, for he learned how to draw plans and charts as well as to make globes. This ability, which impressed two kings among others, together with an unusual curiosity, would have ensured he mastered the latest knowledge and techniques available to Venetian map makers.

Cathay and the Spice Islands first appeared on a Catalan map of 1375 that attempted to incorporate Marco Polo's *Travels* into a graphic representation of European knowledge of the world. Europeans had long known the world was a sphere, but until the 1406 Latin translation of *Geographia* by second-century Alexandrian geographer and mathematician Claudius Ptolemy, they had no means of estimating the earth's circumference or pictorially presenting a spherical world. Ptolemy applied the system of latitude and longtitude developed by Greeks 200 years previously, but he underestimated the earth's circumference by one-fifth. He also held that the known world consisted of a continuous land mass from west to east, broken only by a landlocked sea, the Indian Ocean. Just how close were the extremities of west and east, and whether or not the East could be reached by sailing around Africa or across the Atlantic Ocean (called the "Ocean Sea") became the foremost geographical questions for fifteenth-century map makers and mariners, not least of whom were Columbus and Cabot.

An early attempt to incorporate Ptolemy's world view with Marco Polo's and Conti's reports of the eastern lands was a 1457 Genoese map, which Cabot might have seen or known of. But one map, or versions of it, that Cabot undoubtedly saw was that of his fellow Venetian, the monk Fra Mauro. In 1457 the King of Portugal commissioned Mauro to prepare a world map to show the latest Portuguese discoveries along the West African coast in their search to find a way around the continent to India. After he completed this map (which has not survived) he began to make a copy for the Seignoria of

Venice (which has survived) but he died before its completion. Others finished it, a massive circular planisphere of 6-foot-4-inch diameter carefully coloured on parchment and mounted on wood.

In his world map, Mauro incorporated much detail, including a series of explanatory written legends. As well as having access to the latest Portuguese West African charts, Mauro had Conti's assistance for a lengthy description and graphic portrayal of India and the Spice Islands. Sumatra was shown for the first time, and Japan (Cipangu) probably was as well. All in all, Mauro's map gave Europeans of Cabot's day a greater geographical knowledge of Asia than mid-nineteenth century Europeans would have of central Africa before David Livingstone and others began their explorations of the "dark" continent.

Aside from the wondrous depictions and graphic presentations of the Spice Islands, China, and a fantastically wealthy Cipangu, what would have greatly intrigued Cabot was Mauro's attempt to deal with the geographical relationship of the European and Asian land limits. Mauro shifted his map's centre (and therefore the earth's) farther east from Jerusalem, where previous map makers had placed it to satisfy Christian orthodoxy. By doing so, Mauro got the longitudes of the outer geographical limits of Europe and Asia approximately right. He admitted, however, that he had found contradictory opinions of the earth's true circumference and could not arrive at any definite estimate. So, for any mariner planning to sail west from Europe to reach the East, Mauro's map would not tell him how far he had to sail, a most disconcerting fact at a time when mariners considered 800 miles the farthest limit from land for an ocean voyage.

Opposite: Henricus Martellus' World Map, c. 1490. Cabot likely understood the world's geography much as it is here presented

Chapter Three

VALENCIA

We [King Ferdinand and Queen Isabella] have been informed by Johan Caboto Montecalunya, the Venetian, that he arrived at this city [Valencia] two years ago, and during this time he has considered whether on the beach of this city a port [breakwater ?]could be constructed, and... he has designed and painted plans of them, and he has brought them to us

— The King [Ferdinand of Argon] to Diego de Torres, Governor-General of Valencia, 27 September 1492

Although it is impossible to be certain, in all likelihood Ferdinand's "Johan Caboto Montecalunya" is our John Cabot. (Attempts to decipher "Montecalunya" have met with failure.) Of Roman origin, Valencia lay three miles inland from the Mediterranean on the right bank of the Turia River. Its port, the village of Grao, was at the river's mouth, facing Majorca. When Ferdinand wrote his Governor-General at Valencia about the feasibility of Cabot's plans for a breakwater at Grao, Cabot had apparently been in the city since 1490. Ferdinand's letter and de Torres' reply a month later tell us that Cabot had the ability to both design large projects and obtain a royal audience, where he convincingly presented his ideas using plans he had drawn.

Cabot probably came to Valencia as a merchant-mariner with Venice's 1490 fleet of the Galleys of Barbary, for the city was a centre of the western Mediterranean silk trade. The Galleys of Barbary carried silver and textiles from Venice, stopping at Tunis and other North African ports before crossing to Spain. Once in Valencia, either because his reputation had proceeded him, or, as is most likely, he simply seized the opportunity to impress city authorities with his ability to design a major harbour work, Cabot decided to remain, expecting the breakwater to proceed. Although Ferdinand approved the idea, necessary local financing could not be found and the project was abandoned.

In early April 1493, Columbus passed through Valencia on his triumphal progress to report to Ferdinand and Isabella at Barcelona that he had reached Asia. In August 1492, Columbus had left Spain on his epic voyage to the land of the Great Khan by sailing westwards across the Ocean Sea. As Europeans were to discover during the next two decades of exploration, Columbus had instead found the Americas. Although he would go to his grave believing he had reached Asia, many had their doubts from the first. Among these was John Cabot, who must surely have seen the "High Admiral of the Ocean Sea," richly dressed, with his exotic entourage of frightened bronze-skinned and painted natives from Hispaniola, accompanied by seamen carrying parrots in cages and displaying gold nuggets. Earlier, Columbus had sent an official report to his royal sovereigns, written to prove for any disbelievers that "he had been in the land of Great Khan from which the spices come." As a printed version of the report circulated even before Columbus reached either Valencia or Barcelona, Cabot may have had knowledge of its contents.

Whatever Columbus claimed in his report, with its bombastic language, incredible exaggerations, and, above all, downright lies about gold and spices, Cabot could

Above: Christopher Columbus, attributed to Ridolfo Ghirlandaio

Opposite: Court of King Ferdinand and Queen Isabella at the surrender of the Moorish fortress of Granada. Shortly after its fall the monarchs gave their support to Columbus for his 1492 voyage

have seen little evidence of them as Columbus passed through Valencia. Marco Polo and other travellers had told of a great and powerful empire, large cities of fabled wealth, and harbours filled with ships larger than European vessels. We don't know whether Cabot realized instantly that Columbus had not reached Asia or he arrived at that conclusion later, after others began questioning Columbus' claims. Likely it was a bit of both.

What caused the most doubt among geographers of the day was Columbus' claim that the distance to Asia was "not half what the mathematicians would have it," in short, that the earth's circumference was far less (his estimate was 25 percent less than the correct figure) than the mathematicians had (nearly correctly) calculated. In their view, Columbus must have sailed across 6,000 nautical miles of open ocean to reach the East, which he clearly had not done. No one doubted that Columbus had reached land, but what land was it?

To the sceptical European mind, Columbus could have discovered the "Antipodes" or simply some of the islands map makers loved to distribute across the mysterious Ocean Sea, rather than leave large blank spaces on their creations. Throughout the Middle Ages, Europeans speculated that, in the natural order of things, there should be another continent on the other side of the globe to balance their own. In their imagination they named this continent the Antipodes, from the Greek for two feet planted against each other. By the mid-1400s, scholarly speculation placed this unknown continent out in the Atlantic within the same temperate zone as Europe, just where Columbus had gone.

Antipodean speculation became so widespread among scholars, mariners, and map makers that Cabot could not but have been aware of the theory. It seems, however, to have had no appeal for him. He had become too transfixed on reaching Asia by sailing westwards: an intervening continental land mass would make that impossible. Still, the theory could have influenced his choice of a northern latitude for his 1497 voyage of discovery.

Cabot and others came to believe that Columbus had reached one the islands thought to lie out in the Atlantic that the Portuguese (and also Bristol adventurers, as we shall see) had been searching for. Although the chief thrust of Portuguese exploration lay in seeking to sail around Africa to India, they also sent forth numerous expeditions to explore beyond the Azores to discover other islands they believed must exist in the mid-

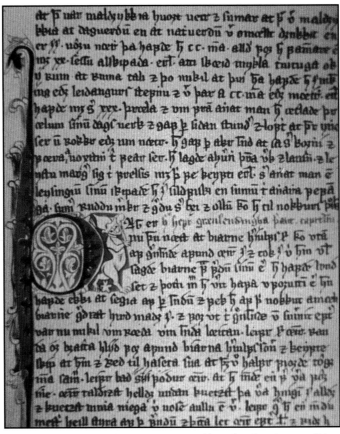

A page from the Greenland Saga

Atlantic. They particularly sought Antillia, the creation of fifteenth-century map makers, who often identified it with another imaginary island, that of the Seven Cities, where legend had it seven bishops and their Christian flocks had fled when the Iberian Peninsula had fallen to the Moorish infidels. Portuguese attempts to push out into the Atlantic to find the mythical Antillia were continually thwarted by the sheer strength of the westerlies that blew across the Atlantic from the Caribbean.

Columbus fully believed in Antillia's existence and hoped to use it as a stopping place on his way, first to Cipangu, and then to the Asian mainland. He crossed the Atlantic where the Portuguese had failed because of his discovery, considered his greatest achievement in navigation, of the mid- and north-Atlantic wind system. Instead of vainly persisting against the westerlies, he went south of the Azores to the Canaries, where he found the northeast trade winds that took him across to the Caribbean. For his return he located the prevailing westerlies that brought him home.

Once Cabot convinced himself that Columbus had reached, not Cipangu or the Asian mainland, but some unknown islands out in the Ocean Sea, he came to believe that he could reach Asia by sailing on a far more northern latitude. As far as we know, by this point Cabot had never sailed outside the Mediterranean, nor had he much opportunity to learn from mariners familiar with Atlantic sailing conditions. His knowledge came from the study of maps and globes, which told him what any mariner or geographer of the day knew, that by sailing on a more northern latitude the distance was shorter. For this to have any practical meaning, however, Cabot had to assume that Asia not only extended into these northern latitudes, but also sufficiently far eastwards so a voyage to the west had a reasonable chance of reaching the land of the Great Khan.

Although Columbus had been virtually alone in believing in a small world, among his contemporaries there were many who shared his other belief that the Asiatic mainland extended much farther eastwards than is the case. This belief formed the basis for Martin Behaim's globe (the oldest terrestrial globe in existence). But because he did not complete his globe until 1492,

neither Columbus nor Cabot could have known of it before Columbus' voyage. His depiction of Asia extending east as far as the longtitude that runs through the centre of Hudson Bay reflected an increasingly accepted view among mariners and geographers. Speculatively at least, Cabot's theory of sailing on a northern latitude made reaching Asia a practical proposition.

In pursuit of his theory, Cabot first sought the backing of the Spanish monarchs and then of King João II of Portugal. Aside from his lack of financial resources, as a private adventurer he could not claim sovereignty over any lands he discovered — for that he needed a royal charter granting him authority to lay claim to his discoveries. As well, only royal patronage could give him the rights and privileges necessary to engage in trade and exercise authority to protect his discoveries from interlopers. Neither Ferdinand and Isabella nor João of Portugal showed the least interest in Cabot and his project, nor was there any reason why they should have. Ferdinand and Isabella believed that Columbus had reached Asia, so it only remained to exploit their good fortune. After Bartholomeu Dias' successful rounding of southern Africa in 1488, Portugal had thrown its resources into finding an eastern sea route to the Spice Islands.

While at Lisbon in his quest for princely support, Cabot seems to have met with English merchants and seamen trading out of Bristol. There was a sufficient meeting of minds and interests between them that Cabot decided that one monarch who might favour his project was King Henry VII.

Chapter Four

BRISTOL

For the last seven years the people of Bristol have equipped two, three [and] four caravels to go in search of the island of Brazil [sic] and Seven Cities according to the fancy of this Genoese

— *Pedro de Ayala to King Ferdinand and Queen Isabella, 25 July 1498*

It is considered certain that the cape of the said land was found [by Cabot on his 1497 voyage] and discovered in the past by the men from Bristol who found 'Brasil' as your lordship well knows

— *John Day to the Lord Grand Admiral c.1497/98*

*J*ohn Cabot, his wife Mattea, and sons Lewis, Sebastian, and Sancio probably arrived at Bristol in late 1494 or early 1495, and could well have come aboard a Bristol merchant's vessel bringing home a cargo of Portuguese wine and fruit. As its ancient Saxon name of Brygstowe ("Place of the Bridge") implies, Bristol had grown up on lands in and around the confluence of two rivers, the Frome and Avon, located some eight miles up the Avon from the Severn Estuary, which flows into Bristol Channel and out to the Atlantic. Bristol's enviable prosperity came from her woolen cloth exports and the importing of wine, much of it fortified and even then named "Bristol

milk," or "Bristol cream sherry" as we call it today. By the 1490s, Bristol, with a population of 10,000, had become the most important English port after London. Her increasingly wealthy and enterprising merchants traded extensively with Ireland, Spain, Portugal, and France.

Above: A late medieval map of Bristol

Opposite: Genealogical tree of Alfonso (1128-1185), the first king of Portugal, by Antonio de Hollanda, showing Lisbon as Cabot would have seen it when he went there around 1494

Cabot would have learned that from the 1430s Bristol fishermen "by needle [compass] and stone [taking

Above: A scene in which the Bristol merchant William Spencer (just left of centre) swears in his successor as the city's Lord Mayor, 29 September 1497. Spencer was one of the backers for the 1480 and 1481 voyages to the west in search of "Brasil"

Opposite: Archaeological excavations at L'Anse aux Meadows

soundings with a lead]" had sailed to Iceland to pursue the fishery, but had been driven out of it by the Hanseactic League. He would have discovered that Bristol's need to replace the Icelandic fishery was the driving force behind attempts to find other islands believed to lie to the west. How much Bristol men knew, or more pertinently, what notions they had, of lands out in the western ocean, remains one of the most intriguing questions surrounding the Cabot story. Columbus likely stopped at Bristol in the late 1470s while reputedly on a voyage to Iceland (and, some would argue, also Greenland) and he might have sailed there in a Bristol vessel.

The oldest tale known in Bristol of westward voyaging and finding land was that of St. Brendan, the sixth-century seafaring Irish abbot. Brendan's voyages to visit his fellow monks in their monasteries from Brittany to the Faroes took the form of a supernatural story of his search for the "Promised Land of the Saints" to the west. Whether or not Brendan or other Irish mariners found the Promised Land across the Atlantic (Newfoundland or Nova Scotia for some) remains highly improbable, but wondrous tales of his voyages became nearly as popular as those of King Arthur and the Holy Grail. A "St. Brendan's Island" appeared on most early maps, though their makers placed it all over the Atlantic from the Gulf of Guinea to Iceland. Every time they sailed, Bristol seamen were reminded of Brendan's search for the Promised Land of the Saints, for they could see overlooking their town Brandon Hill, named in commemoration of a visit made by the saint long ago.

If Brandon Hill and tales of other fabled islands kept alive the notion of land to the west, trading contacts with Iceland could have given Bristol men knowledge of Norse voyaging recorded in the Icelandic sagas. These sagas relate how Erik the Red sailed from Iceland in 982 A.D. to found a colony in Greenland, and that from there members of his family between 1000 and 1020 explored the coasts from Baffin Island possibly as far as Nova Scotia, and that they established a short-lived colony called Vinland. Although the debate over Vinland continues, archaeological and other evidence shows conclusively that, at L'Anse aux Meadows on the northeastern tip of Newfoundland, Norsemen from Greenland established a settlement for trading and exploring within the Gulf of St. Lawrence.

Icelanders maintained communication with Greenland, albeit spasmodically, into the fifteenth century — certainly within the memory of men with whom Bristol fishermen and merchants traded. By the middle of that century, however, contact with Greenland ceased and apparently all knowledge of its settlement was lost until the seventeenth century. There remains a possibility, though any but the most speculative of evidence is lacking, that Bristol seamen found their way to Greenland at some point. Most maps of the day portrayed Greenland as a promontory of northern Europe, though some map makers conceived of it as an island in the western ocean. Whatever their geographical notion of Greenland, Bristol seamen knew of its existence somewhere to the north and west. Of Vinland they might well

have heard from their Icelandic contacts. They at least knew the name, for in his *Itineraries* William Worcestre listed "Wyneland" among King Arthur's conquests. Still, Bristol seamen could not have had any but the very haziest ideas of its location or known whether it was an island or mainland.

What, however, most intrigues historians today about Vinland is how much European map makers knew of the eleventh-century North American discoveries by the Norse, especially in the light of the Vinland Map, believed to date from 1440. Opinion on the authenticity of this map, first presented publicly in 1965 after its procurement by Yale University, has swung from initial general acceptance to non-acceptance — because of scientific findings suggesting it was a fake — back to acceptance again — because of further testing of the ink used. For those who still doubt its authenticity, the issue

of its provenance remains critical, while its ownership history is, to say the least, mysterious.

The map, as the name suggests, shows in the "Ocean Sea" an island to the west and the attached legend "Island of Vinland discovered by Bjarni and Leif in company." Moreover, it has Greenland in recognizable shape as an island and gives a realistic representation of Iceland. Vinland appears as an elongated island a considerable distance to the west and slightly south of Greenland, with two deep jagged inlets that could either be simple conjecture or an attempt to show Baffin Island (in the sagas Helluland) Labrador (Markland) and Newfoundland (Vinland).

Although the Vinland, Greenland, and Iceland part of the map was likely based on Norse charting, the full map seems to have been modelled on a circular world map produced by the Venetian map maker Andrea Bianco, which Cabot must have seen when in Venice. It is believed that the Vinland Map, or the information it imparted, circulated in Italy. If, by chance, Cabot became aware of it while living in Venice, the existence of Vinland would not have so fascinated him as how the map graphically showed the practical possibility of sailing on a northern latitude to Asia, with Vinland no more than an island stopping place. For Cabot and those in Bristol who might have been aware of its existence, Vinland had no greater significance than any of the other islands believed to lie to the west.

Of much greater interest to Cabot would have been the knowledge that some Bristol men had been engaged in a search for the Isle of Brasil, believed to lie west of Ireland. This Isle of Brasil had an even older lineage than Antillia or Seven Cities, first appearing on a 1325 chart. It had no connection to modern Brazil, or the red wood after which that country is named, but meant in Gaelic, "Isle of the Blest." Bristol merchants sent out expeditions "to serch and fynde a certain island called Isle of Brasile" in 1480 and 1481, most probably to find new fishing grounds. The 1480 expedition of a single vessel returned after a fruitless search lasting nine weeks, when driven back by rough

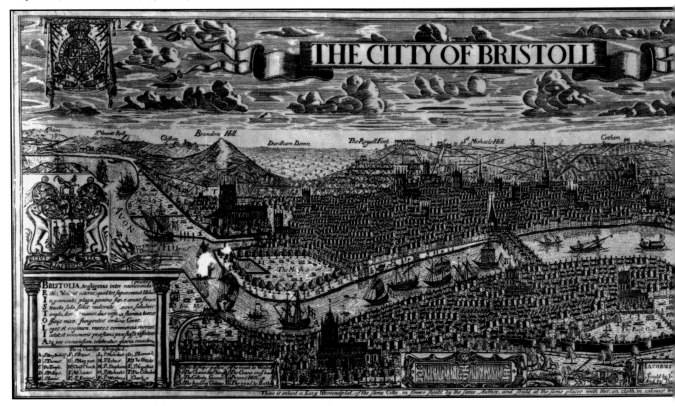

weather. Although it is possible land was found by the 1481 expedition of two ships, the odds are greatly against it. What has stirred speculation is that the ships carried salt for preserving cod, and some believe they might have reached the fishing banks off Newfoundland. If they did, there were no apparent attempts to exploit a fishery, for no record survives of further westward voyaging during the remainder of the 1480s.

This search for the Isle of Brasil could be easily dismissed as an aberration were it not for the testimonies of Pedro de Ayala, the Spanish ambassador, and John Day, an English correspondent of Columbus. De Ayala reported to Ferdinand and Isabella in 1498 that during the early 1490s two to four vessels had gone from Bristol each year to search for Brasil and the Seven Cities. De Ayala could well have deliberately exaggerated the extent of English exploration because he believed this land belonged by right to Spain and he desired to alert his Spanish masters to English intrusions. (Of the John Day letter, more later).

late spring and early summer and then caught the prevailing westerlies, as Columbus learned to do, for the return voyage. There always remains the possibility that whole Isle of Brasil story was no more than a cover for continued illegal fishing off Iceland.

If, however, we accept that some westward voyaging took place before 1497, could Cabot have been in Bristol at that time or have gone on any of them? Almost certainly not, because the evidence has them taking place before his arrival in 1494. Cabot came to

If de Ayala (and Day) reported correctly on voyages to the Isle of Brasil, then just what was going on? The evidence allows for no categorical conclusions. Some historians believe Bristol seamen had discovered America before Columbus, others dismiss this idea outright as no more than seamen's gossip. The most satisfactory explanation for these voyages is that they were fishing expeditions to the Grand Banks off Newfoundland. If so, these Bristol seamen must have worked out the wind pattern for sailing directly west across the North Atlantic and safely returning. They would have used the north-easterlies of

Above: A Parks Canada model of Norse settlement at L'Anse aux Meadows on the northern tip of Newfoundland

Opposite: A 17th century view of Bristol showing Brandon Hill, dedicated to St. Brendan, and the site for the Cabot Tower erected in 1897 as part of Bristol's 400th anniversary commemoration of Cabot's voyage in the Matthew

England because he hoped to secure royal backing and financial support to reach Asia — to do what he believed Columbus had failed to achieve. Whatever the truth of Bristol's search for the Isle of Brasil, there is no evidence of it being associated in English minds with reaching the Spice Islands and fabled Cathay. It was to be Cabot's masterly ability to convince King Henry VII that he could reach Asia and bring to England the spices, silks, and precious stones to be found in the land of the Great Khan that would truly launch England into oceanic discovery in competition with other European maritime powers.

Bristol Castle, which dates from medieval times

Chapter Five

LONDON

*The King, to all to whom, etc. Greeting: Be it
known and made manifest that we have given and
granted... to our well-beloved John Cabot, citizen
of Venice, and to Lewis, Sebastian and Sancio,
sons of the said John... full and free authority, fac-
ulty and power to sail to all parts, regions and
coasts of the eastern, western and northern sea,
under our banners, flags and ensigns*

— *Royal Letters Patent, 5 March 1496*

C abot most likely came to London in late 1495,
the tenth anniversary of Henry VII's founding of
the Tudor dynasty. With his victory on
Bosworth Field on 22 August 1485 and his
marriage to Elizabeth of York a year later,
thereby uniting the Lancastrian and Yorkist
factions and ending the Wars of the Roses,
Henry had brought domestic peace to England.
A cautious, firm, and hard-working ruler, Henry
sought with considerable success to bring orderly government to the country, extend royal authority over unruly
feudal lords, and achieve prosperity for his kingdom. In his
foreign relations, a Spanish alliance became his goal. It was
while negotiations were underway in 1488-89 for a child
marriage between Henry's eldest son, Arthur, and Catherine
of Aragon, daughter of Isabella and Ferdinand, that
Christopher Columbus' brother, Bartholomew, arrived in
England. In his quest for royal patronage, Columbus had
despatched Bartholomew to seek Henry's backing while
waiting in great uncertainty for Ferdinand's and Isabella's
acceptance of his plans for reaching Asia. After many delays,

caused chiefly by his capture and robbery by pirates,
Bartholomew gained an audience with Henry, where he presented his brother's plan using a world map. Bartholomew
spoke no Latin and so probably needed an interpreter, either
one from London's Genoese merchant community or an
Italian diplomat. Domestic affairs and a possible war with
France had too great a claim on Henry's attention for him to
give much thought to backing such speculative ventures as
sailing to Asia. Bartholomew turned to France, where he
also had no success, but by then his brother had finally
gained Spanish backing.

When Cabot arrived in London, uneasy relations pre-
vailed between Henry and Ferdinand over the proposed
marriage of Arthur and Catherine. Largely through the
efforts of the Spanish ambassador, Gonzalez de Puebla, in
whom Henry had great confidence, negotiations
for a marriage treaty were finally concluded.
In his relations with Spain, Henry had to be
conscious of the Treaty of Tordesillas,
signed in 1494 between Spain and
Portugal. That treaty, with the sanction of a
papal bull behind it, divided their respective
spheres of interest along a boundary running
370 leagues west of the Azores. Portugal would
possess lands to the east while Spain could lay claim to
those west of the line.

*A coin commemorating the
marriage in 1486 of Henry VII and
Elizabeth of York*

Cabot could have gained his audience with Henry through the intervention of Bristol merchants or the London Genoese mercantile community. It greatly helped his case that, with Spain's apparent success in reaching Asia, Henry had become receptive to similar proposals so that England would not be left out in the race for the spices and gold of the East. Like Bartholomew Columbus, Cabot probably needed an interpreter. Unlike Bartholomew, however, he had the backing of Bristol merchants who were prepared to finance the venture. Henry, whose frugality was legendary, had no intention of doing so. As well, the fees for obtaining a royal charter could be appreciable and there is no reason to believe Cabot could have paid them himself.

Still, Cabot must have made a most convincing presentation to demonstrate that by sailing west on a northern latitude he could reach northern Asia by a far shorter route than Columbus, who, Cabot believed, had stopped far short of Asia. Cabot had to convince Henry that Asia extended sufficiently far eastwards to make his idea a practical proposition. This is where his knowledge of world maps, gained during his years in Venice, and especially his facility for using globes to present his ideas,

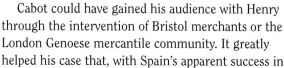

Left: Arthur, son of King Henry VII and Elizabeth of York, and Prince of Wales, c. 1499

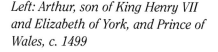

Right: A portrait of Catherine of Aragon, daughter of King Ferdinand and Queen Isabella, by an anonymous artist

must have proven their worth. As well, his experience sailing with the Venetian Galleys of Alexandria and the account of his journey to Mecca to find the source of spices no doubt gave him an eminence no English seaman of the day could match.

Cabot also came to England with a reputation as an expert mariner. He had, however, no extensive experience in ocean navigation, though during his time in Bristol he might well have gone on trading voyages to earn a living. Mediterranean mariners were considerably in advance of their northern colleagues in their use of navigation methods. What most confirmed Cabot's reputation among English mariners was his knowledge of both quadrants and astrolabes to determine latitude, and of the traverse board, a device to help maintain dead reckoning when beating to the windward or whenever forced off an intended course. Marine charts were little used in northern waters, but Cabot, as we have seen, would have used *portolans* extensively while sailing in the Mediterranean. Also, he knew how to draw them for later use by others. In short, though a foreigner with no experience in ocean navigation, Cabot had what no English mariner had — a convincing plan for reaching Asia and its abundant wealth, as well as the navigational knowledge to achieve it.

Once Henry became convinced in principle of Cabot's idea, negotiations on a charter's wording probably took some weeks or months. In drafting the letters patent, royal officials had no precedent to follow: its form and provisions, however, strongly suggest they had before them one of the numerous charters given to Portuguese adventurers seeking new lands. The letters patent were granted to Cabot and his three sons and were valid for their heirs. They gave them the authority to "sail to all parts, regions and coasts of the eastern, western and northern seas under our banners, flags and ensigns." Henry believed he could assuage Spanish sensibilities by barring Cabot from sailing to southern seas, where he might come into conflict with Spain. However, were he to find lands inhabited by "heathens and infidels" unknown to any Christians then living, he was to take possession of them by raising the King's banners, flags, and ensigns. He could possess these lands by occupation or conquest as Henry's vassal and Lord Lieutenant. The implicit two-fold assumption in all this wording was that, once Cabot reached Asia, he could then sail southwest until he came to Cathay, and that Columbus had not got that far, thus giving the rights of discovery to England. The letters patent gave Cabot, his sons, and heirs a monopoly over the trade of any new lands discovered, provided the the King received a fifth of the whole capital gained and Bristol was the port of arrival.

Henry duly signed the letters patent on 5 March 1496. Cabot must have immediately left London, for he sailed that spring from Bristol on a westward voyage. However, disagreements with the crew — presumably on the direction to be taken — shortage of food, and bad weather caused Cabot to return to port. He would have to wait until the following spring and its northeasterlies before attempting another voyage.

The Tower of London with Charles, Duke of Orleans sitting in it. Note the array of shipping

This colourful representation of John Cabot leaving Bristol in May 1497 was done by Ernest Board in 1906. It hangs today in the City of Bristol Museum and Art Gallery

This land was discovered by John Cabot the Venetian, and Sebastian Cabot his son, in the year of the birth of our Saviour Jesus Christ 1494 [misprint for 1497], on the 24th of June in the morning [the Latin version has 5 o'clock in the morning] to which they gave the name First Land Seen [Prima Terra Vista] and to a large island which is near the said land they gave the name Saint John, because it had been discovered on the same day.

— Eighth Legend of the World Map of 1544

Chapter Six
PRIMA TERRA VISTA

*F*or 200 years historians have heatedly debated just where Cabot went on his 1497 voyage. What has bedeviled the debate has been the meagre amount and confusing nature of the available evidence. Not a single record of evidence that can be directly attributed to Cabot has survived. What we have instead are four contemporary reports that cannot be reconciled one with the other, or even with the information given in each. All that can be safely said, without too great a fear of contradiction, is that Cabot left Bristol in a single vessel sometime during May 1497, found new land somewhere between Labrador and the Gulf of Maine, landed once and took possession: he was back in Bristol about 6 August and had an interview with King Henry on or before 10 August.

On 23 August 1497 Lorenzo Pasqualigo, a Venetian merchant in London, wrote his family in Venice with the first report we have of Cabot's voyage. What information it provides is succinct and there is no reason to believe it inaccurate as far as it goes, which is not very far:

> That Venetian of ours who went with a small ship from Bristol to find new islands has come back and says he has discovered mainland 700 leagues [2,240 nautical miles] away, which is the country of the Great Khan, and that he coasted it for 300 leagues [960 nautical miles] and landed and did not see any person... and he has been three months on the voyage; and this is certain. And on the way back he saw two islands, but was unwilling to land, in order not to lose time, as he was in want of provisions.

An unknown London correspondent to the Duke of Milan on 24 August penned the briefest summary we have of the voyage:

> He [Cabot] has returned safe, and has found two large and fertile new islands. He has also discov-
> ered the Seven Cities, 400 leagues [1280 nautical miles] from England, and on the western passage.

Nearly four months later on 18 December, the Duke of Milan's ambassador in London, Raimondo de Soncino, sent a despatch to his master that passed on a little more navigational information than either Pasqualigo or the Duke of Milan's unknown correspondent had provided:

> He [Cabot] started from Bristol... passed Ireland... and then bore towards the north, in order to sail east [to the west], leaving the north [star] on his right hand after some days. After having wandered about for some time he at length arrived at the mainland, where he hoisted the royal standard...

With the above reports, and with whatever information could be gleaned from some of the most enigmatic maps of American discovery known, Cabot historians have had to make do until the discovery of the John Day letter in 1955. It was found by pure chance in the Spanish National Archives, having escaped previous notice because its title cover described it as concerning a presumed English voyage to Brazil, when in reality it referred to Cabot's 1497 voyage and his discovery of the "land found and discovered in the past by the men from Bristol who found 'Brasil.'" As we know, this Brasil had no connection with the South American country, but had been the object of search by Bristol men since 1480. Not only did this letter provide evidence for the previous discovery of America from Bristol, but its detailed description of Cabot's voyage also made it into what the English historian Dr. Alwyn Ruddock called "the most important piece of evidence to come to light in the twentieth century touching the discovery of America." The foremost Cabot scholar of this century, Professor J. A. Williamson, declared its discovery the "most important event in Cabot research during the past one hundred years."

As if the contents of this letter were not explosive enough, that it was sent by an English merchant and addressed to none other than Columbus, using his title of Lord Grand Admiral, added greatly to its scholarly interest and gave it an aura of intrigue. An established

London merchant trading out of Bristol to Spain, John Day became Columbus' chief source on English voyaging. Day promised to report all that came to his knowledge "not prejudicial to the King my master," which has led to suggestions of him being in Spanish pay, or even a double agent. They

Above: A Newfoundland stamp issued to commemorate the 450th anniversary of the Matthew *voyage*

Opposite: Cabot leaving Bristol, painted for 1947 celebrations by Harold Goodridge for the Newfoundland Historical Society. The painting is owned by the Newfoundland government

may have corresponded fairly regularly, as Columbus freely asked Day to procure him such books as a special edition of Marco Polo's *Travels*. Day had the maritime knowledge, and apparently the right connections in both Bristol and London, to provide Columbus with navigational details of Cabot's voyage, including especially critical latitudes, which went well beyond what Pasqualigo and the Duke of Milan's correspondents were able to report. Day wrote his fairly lenghy letter between late December 1497 and March 1498. What follows abstracts the navigational details of Cabot's 1497 voyage:

I am sending... a copy of the land which has been found... I do not send the map because I am not satisfied with it... but from the said copy your Lordship [Columbus] will learn what you wish to know, for in it are named the capes of the mainland and the islands, and thus you will see where land was first sighted, since most land was discovered after turning back. Thus your Lordship will know that the cape nearest Ireland is 1800 miles west of Dursey Head which is in Ireland [latitude 51° 33' N], and the southernmost part of the Island of the Seven Cities is west of the Bordeaux River [the Garonne at latitude 45° 35' N]... They left England toward the end of May, and must have been on the way 35 days before sighting land; the wind was east-northeast and the sea calm going and coming back, except for one day when he ran into a storm two or three days before finding land; and going so far out, his compass needle failed to point north and marked two rhumbs below [that is, north-northwest, a compass variation of 22 1/2°]. They spent about one month discovering the coast and from the above mentioned cape of the mainland which is nearest to Ireland, they returned to the coast of Europe in fifteen days. They had the wind behind them, and he reached Brittany because the sailors confused him [could mean that Cabot had a disagreement with them] saying he was heading too far north.

Bristol seamen relied mostly on the compass and dead

reckoning to find their way in the Atlantic. Day's letter tells us that Cabot used latitude sailing, which required the use of quadrants and astrolabes to determine latitude. A late-medieval quadrant consisted of a thin metal plate in the shape of a quarter circle, with a pair of small sights fixed at right angles to one radial edge and a small weight hung on a line from the circle's centre. An observer aligned the sights with the sun at its noon maximum, or at night with the north star (Polaris) while an assistant read its altitude from the position of the weighted line against a scale of degrees marked on the quadrant's face. Mariners' astrolabes were smaller than those used on land and consisted of a circular metal plate, inscribed with degrees of a circle, pierced with several large openings to lessen wind disturbance. An observer suspended it from a swivel at its top edge and aligned a pair of sights on a rotating pointer with the sun or north star.

Using either of these instruments on a rolling ship was notoriously difficult because of the difficulty in obtaining accurate "heights" from which to determine latitude.

Cabot likely relied on the astrolabe, as de Soncino's letter to the Duke of Milan reports him bearing to the north in order to sail to the west and "leaving the north [star] on his right." Astrolabes were best for reading latitude when using celestial objects high in the sky, which in northern latitudes was the north star. The general rule of thumb for latitude error in Cabot's day was that a reading, if taken on land, could be off by a degree, if taken aboard ship, by as much as two degrees, 140 miles. Day learned of the two latitude readings he sent Columbus directly or indirectly from Cabot. Either or both of them could have been off by as much as two degrees, with significant consequences for determining both Cabot's landfall and where he departed from on his return voyage.

Not until the eighteenth-century invention of the chronometer could mariners determine longitude with any scientific accuracy. They had to rely on their ability to keep course using the compass and to estimate the distance travelled over 24 hours, as measured by a sand-glass turned in half-hour, hour, and four-hour intervals ("a

watch"). As for Pasqualigo's report that Cabot sailed 700 leagues before sighting land and then coasted 300 leagues, we can only treat these figures as very rough estimates. At the same time we can dismiss out of hand the 400-league figure for the Atlantic crossing given by the Duke of Milan's unknown correspondent.

In his Mediterranean sailing, Cabot would not have experienced significant magnetic variation, but as Day's letter tells us, he found the difference between true north and magnetic north to be 22 ½°, which would have been about the declination for Newfoundland in 1500. Day gives no sense that this perturbed Cabot and he may indeed have anticipated it. In short, Day's letter confirms Cabot's abilities as a master mariner.

What none of the contemporary reports tell us is anything about the vessel Cabot sailed in. The first mention of his ship being called the *Matthew* comes from a Bristol chronicle of events written during or after 1576 by Maurice Toby. Toby's chronicle records that the "land of America" was found on St. John the Baptist's Day in 1497 "by the Merchants of Bristowe in a shippe of Bristowe, called the *Mathew*." Bristol Custom records have no record of a *Matthew* before 1492-93, but the records are then missing until 1503-04, when they list a bark *Matthewe*, so the accepted assumption is that the *Matthew* was built or acquired between 1493 and 1497. Cabot's wife's name was Mattea and he could have named the vessel after her: there is no feminine in English for Matthew,

and so an anglicized Mattea became Matthew.

Although we have no description of the *Matthew*, it is generally believed that she was a typical weatherly three-masted bark of 50 tons. By Cabot's time, European shipwrights and seamen had developed such vessels because of their ability to sail well into the wind and their seaworthiness for ocean sailing. Cabot recruited a crew of twelve to fourteen. Also sailing on the *Matthew* were two or more unknown Bristol merchants, a Burgundian, and a Genoese barber [likely as a surgeon] and possibly Cabot's son Sebastian, for a crew total of between eighteen and twenty.

Cabot and the *Matthew* left Bristol (51° 20' N) sometime in the latter half of May. The most extraordinary aspect of the navigational information given in John Day's letter is that it is open to two entirely opposing interpretations of the latitude Cabot followed in crossing the Atlantic, his landfall, and where he went on his coasting voyage. For convenience I divide the proponents of these two theories into the Bristol and Morison Schools of historians. Both agree that the *Matthew* made a good run from Bristol in a calm sea with an east-northeast wind, as Day tells us, for 31 or 33 days, that is until 21 or 22 June, when she ran into a storm. At this point Cabot's compass showed a variation of 22 ½°. They also agree that Cabot sighted land on the morning of 24 June (in the Julian calendar used in Cabot's time, but in ours, the Gregorian, 3 July) Saint John the Baptist's Day. Nor is there any significant disagreement on the reports of Cabot's going ashore with a small party near where he first sighted land. After landing, he erected a wooden cross and took ceremonial possession by raising banners with the arms of Henry VII and Pope Alexander VI on them, though Pasqualigo, the Venetian correspondent, has him raising those of St. Mark of Venice and of England, but makes no mention of the Pope. Being small in number and fearing possible attack, the landing party did not go inland beyond a crossbow shot. They found a trail and discovered such evidence of human habitation as a site where a fire had been made,

Cabot would have used a quadrant similar to this one to determine his latitude.

snares set for animals, manure they believed came from farm animals, and a stick half a yard long pierced at both ends, carved and painted with brazil (red ochre). They noted particularly that there were tall trees suitable for making masts, and fertile grasslands. Although none of the reports of the voyage have Cabot attempting to determine latitude while ashore, both schools assume that he did, though the results would have been dependent on how well he could see the sun at noon.

Because there is no agreement on Cabot's landfall, there is equally none on where he went on his month-long coasting voyage, but both schools generally agree with the reports of what happened on it. After taking on water, Cabot took the *Matthew* coasting southwards for a time during which sailors thought they saw humans running in the woods, but Cabot was not to land again. Pasqualigo reports that he became concerned about a shortage of provisions and did not wish to waste time in making landings, though Day reports that he had sailed with enough food for seven or eight months. Day also says the *Matthew* now spent a month coasting, and that "most of the land was discovered after turning back." Cod appeared in such abundance that the crew could lower buckets weighted with stones to catch them.

Both schools agree that Cabot sailed for home around 24 July "from the cape nearest Ireland" and "1800 miles west of Dursey Head," that is from near Cape Bauld. The *Matthew* made an incredibly fast passage of fifteen days,

though the crew held that she was sailing too far north and Cabot changed to a more southerly course that brought them to Brittany. By about 6 August the *Matthew* was back in Bristol, and four days later Cabot had got to London, where he told King Henry and all who would listen that he had reached Asia.

The Bristol School's origins are in two generations of scholarly research into Bristol's place in the history of early English maritime expansion, especially possible pre-Cabot voyages of discovery. For Cabot's 1497 voyage, the Bristol School has the *Matthew* sailing southwest on the latitude of Bordeaux, France near the mouth of the Garonne River at 45° 35' N, where Cabot expected to find the Isle of Brasil or Seven Cities. As Day records, after a good run west across the Atlantic, she ran into a storm. At this point, Cabot's compass showed a variation of 22 ½°, which it is believed he probably corrected for, and the *Matthew* was being pushed south by the Labrador Current. This likely happened somewhat east of Newfoundland or over the Grand Banks. After two or three days, the storm ended and land was sighted on 24 June. The combination of the southward force of the

Top left: This brass nocturlabe or "star-dial," dates from the 16th century. Nocturlabes were used to calculate time at night using the north star

Above: Canadian four-cent stamp, 1949

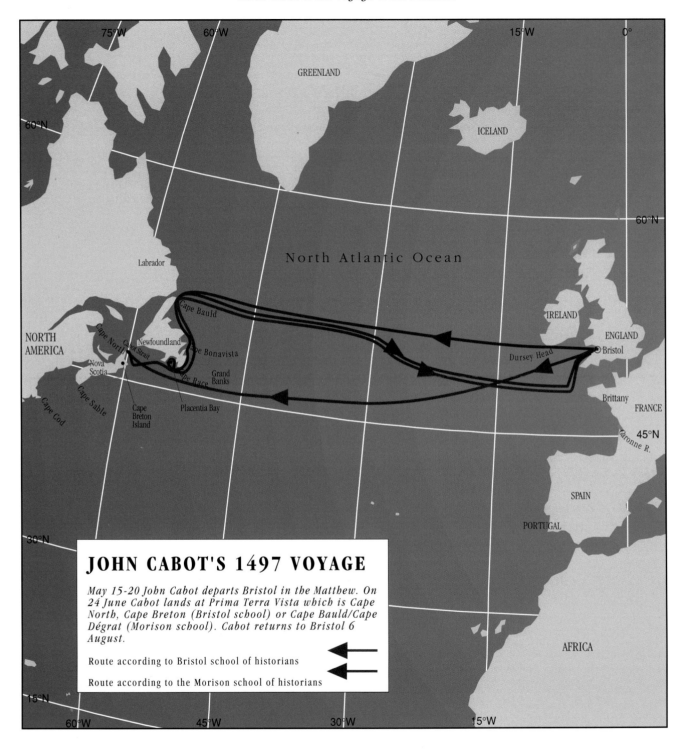

JOHN CABOT'S 1497 VOYAGE

May 15-20 John Cabot departs Bristol in the Matthew. On 24 June Cabot lands at Prima Terra Vista which is Cape North, Cape Breton (Bristol school) or Cape Bauld/Cape Dégrat (Morison school). Cabot returns to Bristol 6 August.

Route according to Bristol school of historians

Route according to the Morison school of historians

Labrador Current and the storm had driven the *Matthew* past Newfoundland, without any land being sighted. The first land sighted was a headland of Cape Breton Island in the area of 45° 57' N. An error by Cabot in taking latitude could, however, put the landfall anywhere between Cape Sable and Cape Race. For Cabot's month-long coasting voyage, the Bristol School has him sailing across the Cabot Strait and then north along the Newfoundland coast to the Dursey Head latitude.

An outward voyage on the Garonne River latitude, as argued by the Bristol School, is dismissed as "untenable" by the American maritime historian, Samuel Eliot Morison. Morison holds that Cabot left Bristol on 20 May and headed for Dursey Head in Ireland, from where the *Matthew* turned westwards and held to that latitude in the hope of reaching Cathay on a high, short latitude. In compelling prose, Morison uses graphic nautical language to describe what he, admittedly, imagines Cabot did as he began "to feel 'the loom of land' — the odor of fir trees and other growing things floating out over the sea, low-hanging clouds, gannets, guillemots, and other non-pelagic [sic] birds flying and screaming." Cabot then

took soundings and found land under the *Matthew*'s keel. At last, "At 5:00 a.m. the rugged mass of Newfoundland's northern peninsula rises out of the sea, dead ahead, distant twelve to fifteen miles." Morison believes that Cape Dégrat was sighted before Cape Bauld and that Cabot landed at the former, only five miles as the crow flies from

Top: From the John Cabot mural painted by Lewis Parker, now at the University College of Cape Breton

Opposite: This map shows how the Bristol and Morison Schools of historians differ on Cabot's ourward course and explorations during his 1497 voyage

L'Anse aux Meadows, the site of the Greenland Norse settlement of 500 years earlier. Either in a quiet anchorage or ashore, Cabot took latitude readings by day by the sun and at dawn and evening by the north star, working them out as the approximate latitude of Dursey Head at 51° 33' N. As that of Cape Dégrat is 51° 37' N, Morison says that this must be "considered one of the most accurate and successful bits of celestial navigation in the early history of discovery." However, as already noted, Cabot's latitude

*Above: Enactment of Cabot landing at
Cape North, Cape Breton*

*Opposite: When Cabot visited London
in 1496 it would have looked very
much as in this map of c.1560*

could have been in error by as much as two degrees on either side, which could have meant a Labrador or Cape Bonavista landfall.

For the coasting voyage as outlined in Day's letter, Morison has Cabot go south past Cape Bonavista, St. John's Harbour, and Cape Race and then "turning the corner" into Placentia Bay, his farthest southward voyaging at latitude 46° 37' N — just a few miles north of the Bordeaux latitude given by Day as the southernmost land visited by Cabot. Cabot then returned to his landfall opposite Dursey Head and on 20 July headed home to Bristol.

What are we to make of these two completely contrary arguments that use the same basic evidence from Day's letter? Both schools agree that Cabot returned to Bristol on the Dursey Head latitude, that is from Cape Bauld. Where they fundamentally disagree is in their interpretation of Day's statement that "from said copy of land which has been found... your Lordship [Columbus] will learn what you wish to know, for in it are named the capes of the mainland [the cape on the Dursey Head latitude] and the islands [the cape on the southernmost part of the Island of the Seven Cities on the Bordeaux River latitude], and thus you will see where land was first sighted, *since most of the land was discovered after turning back* [my italics]."

The Bristol School interprets this wording to mean that Cabot first sighed land near the southernmost cape, while Morison builds his whole case around the Dursey Head latitude. Morison also finds it inconceivable that the *Matthew* could have made a Cape Breton landfall without first sighting Newfoundland, and this is certainly a major difficulty in accepting a Cape Breton landfall. There is considerably greater difficulty, however, with Morison's statement that Cabot sailed from Cape Bauld all the way to Placentia Bay and then retraced his course back to Cape Bauld, especially in the light of Day's statement, that "most of the land was discovered after turning back." Day also reports that on landing Cabot found tall trees of the kind masts are made from. As neither black spruce nor white pine are found as far north as Cape Bauld, this suggests a more southerly landfall. In general, the Bristol School's case adheres far better to Day's letter than does Morison's.

Chapter Seven

LONDON AND RETURN TO ASIA

This yeere [1498] the king caused to man and victuall a shippe at Bristowe, to search for an Ilande, which hee [Cabot] saide hee knewe well was riche and replenished with riche commodities. Which Ship, thus manned and victualed at the Kinges cost, divers merchants of London ventured in her small stocks, being in her chief Patrone of the saide Venetian. And in the companie of the saide shippe sayled also out of

Bristowe three or four small ships fraught with sleight and grosse merchandizes, as course cloth, Caps, Laces, points, and other trifles, and so departed from Bristowe in the beginning of May: of whom in this Maiors [William Purchas, Mayor of London] time returned no tidings

— *Chronicle of Robert Fabyan for the year 1498 as rendered by Richard Hakluyt in his* Divers Voyages, *1582 edition*

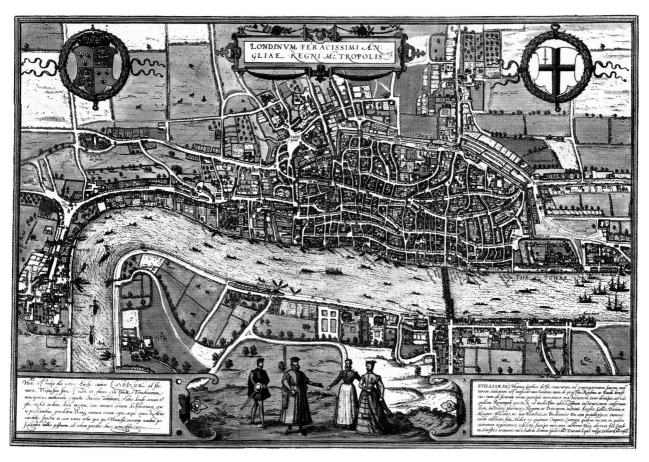

Cabot returned to England in the summer of 1497 to great acclaim and honour. Pasqualigo reported with pride on his fellow Venetian, who was now being called "Great Admiral" and went about London dressed in silk with English and Venetian rogues running after him like mad. At court, King Henry was openly pleased with Cabot's discovery and bestowed £10 upon "hym that found the new isle." This reference to "new isle" could have been simply a clerk's wording, but it does raise the question of what people believed Cabot had discovered. Some, like Day, believed it was the Isle of the Seven Cities, and they may or may not have associated this land with Asia. Pasqualigo seems to have spoken with Cabot, and his report is emphatic that he had discovered mainland, "which is the country of the Grand Khan." This might be what the King thought as well, for he promised Cabot ten armed ships for the following spring and apparently more money. With that Cabot had to be satisfied for the

moment, because Henry had domestic rebellion and war with Scotland to deal with, neither of which was resolved until December.

Early in December, Cabot had the opportunity, likely at Henry's court, to give a public description of his voyage. For this he had with him some of his companions, presumably some of those Bristol merchants who went on the voyage. Cabot used a world map and a globe he had made to explain where he had been. His Bristol companions testified he spoke the truth. They also spoke in glowing terms of the cod fishery they had found, which was so abundant that the English would have no further need of Iceland. Cabot used this opportunity to expound on his plan to return to the newly discovered land, which he held was eastern Asia, and then follow the coast southwest until he reached Cipangu in the equinoctial region, where he believed all the spices originated and precious stones could also be found. Henry was so impressed that he granted Cabot a yearly pension of £20 to be taken from Bristol Customs revenues and issued a second letter patent authorizing him to impress six English ships, paying for them at the King's rates of three pence per ton per week. Henry promised to equip ships and give Cabot prisoners from the gaols to establish a colony in the distant land, as the Venetians had at Alexandria, and so make London into a great mart for the spice trade. There was much excitement because the prospects for great wealth seemed at hand. Cabot thought of himself as a prince. He bestowed islands on companions from the first voyage and also promised bishoprics to some

As an expert mariner, Cabot would have had the astronomical knowledge depicted in this celestial globe, which dates from 1533. The constellations appear as gods and animals

poor friars who were to accompany him on the second.

The expedition that left Bristol in early May of 1498 consisted of five vessels, one of which Henry had provided with crew and weapons. They carried provisions for a year, with London and Bristol merchants supplying the cargo of trading goods and financing the voyage. In July, a report from Ireland told of the fleet running into a gale. One ship, which may or may not have been Cabot's, had to put into an Irish port for repairs before continuing westwards. This is the last surviving record we have of the fleet. Of John Cabot's fate, the last word we have comes from Polydore Vergil, who wrote in a manuscript copy of his *Anglica Historia*, written in 1512-13, that Cabot set sail for the west and "he is believed to have

found the new lands nowhere but on the very bottom of the ocean, to which he is thought to have descended together with his boat, the victim of that self-same

Knights and Ladies Ride Out to a Tournament in London, *from Friossart's* Chronicle *of the late 15th century*

ocean; since after that voyage he was never seen again anywhere." His pension from Henry was last drawn for the year 1498-99, presumably by his widow Mattea, of whom no more has ever been found.

Yet, it would have been most unusual in the annals of early European voyages of discovery for no vessel in a fleet of five to return. There is some circumstantial evidence about what might have happened. In 1501, two vessels of a Portuguese expedition, sent out under the command of Gaspar Corte-Real to explore lands in the western Atlantic, arrived back in Lisbon. One of the ship's crew brought back a piece of a broken gilt sword and a pair of silver earrings obtained from Indians. Both seemed to be of Italian manufacture. As the expedition had voyaged nearly to Hudson Strait before coasting down the Labrador, Newfoundland, and Nova Scotia coasts, they could have found the broken sword and earrings anywhere. Still, they must have come from one of Cabot's voyages. On the 1497 voyage Cabot had landed only once and then for a short time, which leaves the 1498 voyage. Of the five vessels of that second expedition, at least one probably made a successful crossing. Indians could have obtained the sword and earrings by barter or possibly as the result of a skirmish. The Portuguese kidnapped 57 Indians of the Newfoundland Beothuk tribe and brought them to Lisbon as slaves, so the crew may have obtained the broken sword and earrings while ashore. Corte-Real also made at least one other landing, on either Cape Breton Island or mainland Nova Scotia.

Cabot's plan, after reaching the land discovered in 1497, was to sail southwest into the tropical regions where he believed Cipangu lay. As we have noted, Spain did not look favourably on Cabot's voyages and its ambassador voiced his concerns to King Henry. Somehow the Spanish came to believe that English ships had reached as far south as the Isthmus of Panama. A 1499 Spanish expedition under the command of Alonso de Hojeda may have encountered English ships in the Caribbean. These could only have been part of Cabot's expedition. De Hojeda spent the voyage "killing, robbing and fighting," so the fate of any English he came across can be readily imagined.

It also remains possible that one of Cabot's vessels that coasted southwards did return to Bristol. If so, she could have carried back news that the land discovered on the 1497 voyage could not be Asia because there were no great cities, no Cipangu or Spice Islands to be found where Cabot said they were. Such a report could explain why, from 1498 onward, there was no more talk about the land of the Grand Khan or of London becoming a great mart for spices. After that date we read only of "the New Land" or "the New Found Land."

The disastrous 1498 voyage did not, however, quench interest in the land Cabot had found on his 1497 voyage. A series of subsequent Portuguese and English voyages explored the new land. Little is known of them, especially those sent out from Bristol in the years 1502, 1503, 1504, and 1505. These confirmed the abundance of the fishery and that the new land was not Asia. The Portuguese benefitted most from these voyages by firmly establishing a seasonal fishery on the Grand Banks. For reasons not entirely clear, Bristol merchants did not pursue this fishery, leaving it to the Portuguese, the French, and the Basques. There was, however, one last voyage of discovery from Bristol in 1508 that sailed with Sebastian Cabot in command. Still dreaming of the riches of the East, Sebastian sought a passage to Asia through the great land mass that Europeans were coming to realize was a continent, a New World.

Chapter Eight
SEBASTIAN CABOT

Furthermore, Sebastian Gabota, by his personall experience, and travell, hath set foorth, and described this passage, in his Charts, whiche are yet to bee seene, in the Queenes Majesties [Elizabeth I] privie Gallerie at White hall, who sent to make his discoverie by King Henrie the seaventh, and entred the same fret [strait]... and finding the Seas still open, said, that he might, and would have gone to Cataia [Cathay] if the Mutinie of the Maister & Mariners, had not ben.

— Sir Humphrey Gilbert, A Discourse of a Discoverie for a new Passage to Cathaia *(London, 1576, written before 1566)*

*O*f John and Mattea Cabot's three known sons, only the wily Sebastian has survived in the historical record. Of him we know much more than of his father, but this has not lessened the controversy surrounding this second of John Cabot's sons. To start with, Sebastian gave four differing dates for his birth. Sebastian probably did not know when he was born. One claim by him of English birth was a self-serving attempt late in life to gain English nationality at a time when he feared being extradited to Spain. Although the exact date of his birth remains unknown, it can be safely put at a year or two before 1484 and in Venice. This would make him thirteen to fifteen years old when John Cabot sailed in 1497. As the author of the eighth legend in his 1544 map, Sebastian claimed to have been co-discoverer with his father of the land they named *Prima Terra Vista.* But

Sebastian also went further, or is recorded as having done so, by proclaiming himself the sole discoverer.

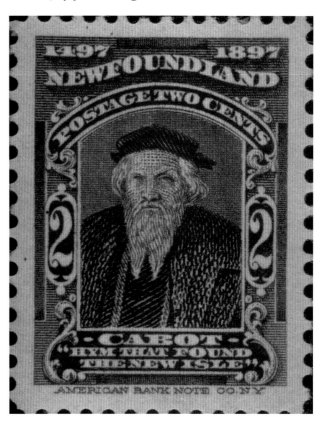

Although this stamp was issued for the 1897 Cabot Commemoration, the picture is not of John Cabot, but of Sebastian. It comes from a copy made in 1838 for the Massachusetts Historical Society of an original painting that was later destroyed in a fire

The Venetian historian of discovery, Giovanni Battista Ramusio, corresponded with Sebastian. In his noted work *Navigationi et Viaggi*, first published in 1550, he included a story of a house-party near Verona he had attended around 1544. A "Mantuan gentleman," whose name he withheld "out of respect," described for the guests an interview he had had sometime before with Sebastian in Seville, who was then in Spanish employ. What Sebastian reportedly told the gentleman has remained among the most tantalizing stories about the Cabots. Sebastian said his father had left Venice many years before and settled in London as a merchant. Although Sebastian was very young, he had studied the humanities and the sphere. His father, according to Sebastian, had died about the time the English court heard about Columbus' wonderful discovery. Feeling the desire to achieve something equally great, Sebastian convinced Henry VII by means of a globe that there was a shorter route westwards to the Indies. The King furnished him with two ships and he sailed in 1496 (or 1497) expecting to reach Cathay and then proceed to India. The coast he came to trended northwards and he followed it, looking for a westward passage. Unsuccessful, he turned away away and searched southwards as far as "Florida" — the name given in the sixteenth century to all the eastern American seaboard. And so ends the gentleman's story.

Ramusio's tale was not to be the last crediting Sebastian with voyages made by his father. In 1580, John Stow published *The Chronicles of England From Brute unto this present yeare of Christ*. A humble tailor until he was 40 years old, Stow became an avid chronicler and assiduous researcher into English archives. (In 1603, no longer able to work and in dire need, James I allowed him by royal patent the privilege of begging his bread under the porches of all churches.) Stow's source for a voyage by Sebastian Cabot was a manuscript chronicle by Robert Fabyan. Transcribing a Fabyan entry for 1498, Stove wrote that Sebastian had led the Cabot expedition. In both Ramusio's tale and Stow's entry we can recognize aspects of the 1497 and 1498 voyages, but with Sebastian receiving the credit due his father. Sebastian's detractors cite these as examples of the son's disingenuousness.

After his father failed to return from the 1498 voyage, Sebastian seems to have stayed in Bristol and learned the mariner's trade, possibly sailing with some of the expeditions sent out from Bristol from 1502 to 1505. His activities came to Henry VII's notice, who in 1505 awarded to "Sebastian Caboot Venycian" a pension of £20 "in consideracion of the diligent service and attendaunce" rendered to the King in and about Bristol. It is possible, of course, that John Cabot's death was finally accepted and his pension was now to be paid to the family in the name of Sebastian.

Sebastian inherited his father's talent for convincing others of his abilities and the practicality of his ideas. He also inherited his father's fixation with finding Cathay. Sebastian was able to convince Henry and some English merchants to finance a voyage to discover a way through or around the "new found land" and thereby reach Cathay. In the spring of 1508, with two ships under his command, Sebastian sailed by way of Iceland and southern Greenland to the Labrador coast. From this landfall he went north and west, but his crew became so fearful of the ice that they refused to go farther into what seems unquestionably to have been Hudson Strait and Bay. Sebastian then sailed south, probably coasting down as far as Chesapeake Bay, where he wintered before returning home in the spring of 1509. To his dying day, Sebastian believed he had found a passage to Cathay, and this appeared on maps he later drew, but are now lost.

With this voyage, interest in England waned for further exploration. Sebastian turned to map making for a living. While in Spain with an English army preparing to invade France in 1512, Sebastian took employment with the Spanish service. In 1515 he became "Pilot to His Majesty" and three years later received the office of Pilot-Major. As Pilot-Major, Sebastian held responsibilities for instruction in navigation and instrument making, the examination and licencing of pilots, the scrutiny and correction of official charts, and the compilation of hydrographic information. These duties gave him an important role in Spanish overseas affairs. It was through this role that Sebastian obtained command in 1526 of a Spanish expedition for the discovery of "Eastern Cathay" by finding a passage through South America in the River Plate region. He left with a fleet of four vessels and 200 men and returned in 1530 with one ship and 24 men: all he could show for his efforts were 50 Indian slaves purchased just before his return. This disaster did little for his reputation as an explorer. His abilities lay far more in his map making.

During his Spanish service, Sebastian engaged in numerous intrigues with Venetian and English authorities, though with no discernable benefit to himself. As early as 1538 he sought English employment, but not until 1547 did he return to England, where he received an annuity of £166 from King Edward VI. Spain called, unsuccessfully, for his extradition as a "verie necessary man" to the Emperor Charles V, whose servant he was. In England, Sebastian again took up his dream of a passage to Cathay, but now to the northeast. He prepared the instructions for expeditions sent by the Muscovy Company. When, aged 74, he went to Gravesend in 1556 to see one of these expeditions off, he entertained the ship's company at an inn by entering into the "dance himselfe amongst the rest of the young and lusty company." He died the following year.

Henry VII's letters patent of 5 March 1496 were granted to John Cabot and to his sons, Lewis, Sebastian, and Sancio, "and to heirs and deputies of them." John Cabot could possess as a vassal of the King any new lands he found and enjoy all the profits from them. Sebastian considered himself heir to all his father's discoveries and took pains to keep this claim valid. Any children of his could lay claim as well. He married twice, had at least one daughter, but it seems no sons. Although claims have been made, no descent from him has been proven, and so with Sebastian's death the Cabot line ended in England.

Chapter Nine

ENIGMATIC MAPS

This Messer Zoane [John Cabot] has the description of the world in a map, and also in a solid sphere, which he has made, and shows where he has been.

— Raimondo de Raimondi de Soncino to the Duke of Milan, 18 December 1497

Soon after de Soncino wrote of Cabot's map, John Day also mentioned a map in a letter to Columbus, which he did not enclose because he was not satisfied with it. He had, however, hurriedly made a copy of it and this he sent with his letter. From the copy, Day said that Columbus would be able to see where land was first sighted, that "the cape nearest to Ireland" was 1,800 miles west of Dursey Head, and that the southernmost part of the "Island of Seven Cities" was west of the Bordeaux River. When Pedro de Ayala wrote Ferdinand and Isabella in July of 1498, he told them that he had also seen the map made by Cabot.

Opposite: Juan de la Cosa's map of 1500 or possibly a few years later was the first to show English discoveries. La Cosa is believed to have obtained his information from a sketch made by John Cabot during his 1497 voyage

He assumed his sovereigns already knew the results of Cabot's 1497 voyage and wrote of a chart, or world map, that Cabot had made, and which was apparently in de Ayala's possession, though he did not send it at that time. De Ayala and his Spanish masters believed that the lands discovered by Cabot were those already found for Spain by Columbus. Clearly, Spain had a very direct and immediate national interest in where Cabot had been, and expected to receive more details, as did Columbus, in the form of maps and charts.

In 1832 one Baron Walckenaer found an old map in a Paris curio shop. On reading the description, *Juan de la Cosa la fizo en el Puerto de S. Ma. en año de 1500* ("Juan de la Cosa made this at Puerta de Santa Maria in the year 1500") he realized he was looking at a *mappemonde*, or world map, with a very early depiction of the Americas' coastline. After Walckenaer's death in 1853, an agent for the Queen of Spain purchased it at auction. Today, it is one of the treasures of the Spanish Naval Museum in Madrid. La Cosa was Columbus' cartographer on his second voyage of 1493, and possibly on others. He also sailed with Alonso de Hojeda in 1499, when de Hojeda might have encountered vessels of Cabot's ill-fated 1498 voyage.

La Cosa drew his map on oxhide, measuring three feet by six feet. It is, in fact, two separate maps, one of the Old World portraying Europe, Africa and Asia, and a western section in a half-moon shape showing what appears to be the coastline from Greenland south to Cuba and northern South America. This is the earliest known representation of the Americas' continental coastline incorporating the new discoveries of the previous decade. The two maps are joined together at a meridian running through the Atlantic Ocean and are drawn to different scales, with the western half much larger, though la Cosa treated them as if they were to one scale. Also, the halves are of two different dates, the western half being later than the eastern. Many of the names given to land features are not recognizable in any language, while others have become indecipherable because of the map's degeneration over the years. The map appears to have been drawn in freehand, with the draftsman copying from charts and other maps, which were themselves in all likelihood freehand copies. The result is a more elongated and unindented coastline than was likely portrayed in the original charts or maps copied.

No map of western discovery has been more studied, nor proven more enigmatic, than la Cosa's. Opinions on it vary widely. S. E. Morison, for instance, dismissed it as no more than a Spanish compliment to the newly crowned Henry VIII on his marriage to Catherine of Aragon and claimed it was drawn by la Cosa around 1509 (though he provided no evidence for this other than an imaginary conversation between King Ferdinand and la Cosa). Others hold that it reveals the course of Cabot's coasting during his 1497 voyage.

On the northern part of the map's western half runs a fairly straight coastline from west to east. Five English flags are marked on this coastline, with such names as *cauo de ynglaterra* ("Cape of England") and *cauo descubierto* ("Cape Discovery") given to particular land features,

and the words *mar descubierta por ingliese* ("sea discovered by the English"). Those who accept the 1500 date and the map's authenticity argue with considerable credibility that la Cosa must have had before him a copy of Cabot's survey or chart made while he coasted during his 1497 voyage, that the copy probably came to him via John Day and Columbus, or possibly through de Ayala. To most observers, the east-west orientation of the "English Coast" eliminates it as a possible representation of Labrador and Newfoundland's northeastern coast. For them, it portrays part or all of the coast roughly on a general line from Cape Sable across Cabot Strait (which is not shown) to Cape Race. Endless attempts to relate la Cosa's "English Coast" to the actual topography has produced no consensus and is unlikely to do so.

David Quinn of the Bristol School of Cabot historians, however, in his 1974 work, *England and the Discovery of America*, puts forward an intriguing and quite convincing argument reconciling Day's letter with la Cosa's map. His basic contention is that la Cosa had no more than a very sketchy plan of Cabot's coasting that was without scale and gave only latitudes for landfall and departure. La Cosa put the most western of the English flags (the point of land is

The only surviving copy of Sebastian Cabot's 1544 world map. A copy hung for years in Whitehall Palace, where Richard Hakluyt and Sir Humphrey Gilbert, among others, saw it. Note the words prima tierra iusta *on the headland that is unmistakably Cape Breton at the entrance to the Gulf of St. Lawrence, with Newfoundland appearing as a group of islands*

not named) where, on the Bordeaux latitude, appear the words *mar descubierta por ingliese*. Quinn argues that this was Cabot's landfall and that the most eastern of the flags, at *cauo de ynglaterra*, which is on the Dursey Head latitude, was Cabot's point of departure. La Cosa then copied as best he could, in a more or less a straight line towards the northeast, Cabot's undoubtedly sketchy survey between the two latitudes. The phrase *mar descubierta por ingliese* might refer to Cabot Strait or more generally to the waters between northern Cape Breton and Newfoundland.

At best, la Cosa's map provides us with evidence of Spanish recognition for Cabot's discoveries in these latitudes of the "English Coast." La Cosa seems to have had no more than the Dursey Head and Bordeaux latitudes to work with and only a rough sketch of the land found on Cabot's coasting voyage. As for Cabot's landfall, it suggests a southern rather than a northern *prima terra vista*. A 1544 map by Sebastian Cabot is, however, more explicit: it cites Cape Breton as the first land seen, though it has proven to be as controversially enigmatic as la Cosa's map.

Like la Cosa's map, the 1544 map was a fortuitous nineteenth-century discovery, but, unlike la Cosa's, it was previously known to have existed. In 1582, Richard Hakluyt, in his *Divers Voyages touching the Discovery of America,* reprinted a variant of the eighth legend on the 1544 map. He likely saw the copy that in his day hung at Westminster Palace. A schoolmaster to the King's Henchmen at Greenwich, Clement Adams, re-engraved the map in 1549, and Hakluyt may also have used this version. These and all other copies then disappeared until the rediscovery of a single copy in a Bavarian priest's house in 1843, when the French Government purchased it for the Bibliothèque Nationale.

While at Seville as Pilot-Major, Sebastian contracted in 1541 with two German printers for the production of a world map, which was printed in the Netherlands three years later. On the map were a number of descriptive legends, separately printed and pasted on, in Spanish and Latin. It appears from the map's typography that the legends were originally written in Spanish and then translated into Latin by the Dutch publishers. There is general agreement that this map is of inferior quality, a commercial venture, based on a 1541 French map by Nicolas Deslien, but there is no consensus on how much involvement Sebastian had in its production. Because much of the work took place in the Netherlands, Sebastian likely could not have supervised it beyond its initial drafting stage and would not have seen the final result.

The eighth legend of the 1544 map states: "This land was discovered by John Cabot the Venetian and Sebastian Cabot his son, in the year of the birth of our Saviour Jesus Christ 1494 [misprint for 1497] on the 24th of June in the morning, to which they gave the name Land First Seen [in the Latin version *prima terra vista* and in the Spanish *prima tierra vista*]." On the map, where Cape Breton is unmistakably located, are the words in Spainish *prima tierra uista* (misprint for *vista*), but the legend itself does not state where *prima tierra vista* was. It goes on to describe the people of the land as dressed in animal skins and inhabiting a very sterile land with many white bears and very large stags like horses.

"Land First Seen" obviously relates to John Cabot's 1497 voyage, while the subsequent description derives from a voyage to Labrador where, as we know, Sebastian is believed to have sailed in 1508. The 1544 map has long been a mainstay for those adhering to a Cape Breton landfall. Those holding for a Newfoundland landfall have dismissed its relevance on the grounds that, a): Sebastian was an unmitigated liar (a bit strong, but not without truth) b): Sebastian wrote *prima tierra vista* by Cape Breton because it was believed at the time to be mainland and Cabot wanted to show that England had first discovered the North American mainland because he was then seeking English employment; and c): Sebastian had a faulty memory or was simply confused.

Whether or not Sebastian accompanied his father on the 1498 voyage, he would have seen his father's charts and maps. Because he learned cartography early in life, probably first of all from his father, he could have assisted in their preparation, and he would have certainly understood them. In his later years, Sebastian is known to have kept numerous maps and papers in his house. After his death, custody of these passed to a William Worthington and they later disappeared without a trace. When Hakluyt, however, published his 1582 *Divers Voyages*, he included a map of the Atlantic drawn by Michael Lok. On this map, Lok showed a "C. Bretou" with the inscription: "J. Gabot. 1497." Sebastian must have been Lok's source, directly or indirectly. If Sebastian was deliberately lying, there would have been some still alive who could have disputed both his claim to have accompanied his father and a Cape Breton landfall. The *prima terra vista* statement and the marking of Cape Breton have a definitiveness to them that cannot be easily dismissed on such grounds as faulty memory or sheer political opportuntism.

CONTROVERSY AND COMMEMORATION

In the controversy which has gone on for years as to the first land seen by Cabot and his son whether the coast of Labrador, or the northeastern cape of Cape Breton, or Cape Bonavista or some other headland on the eastern shores of Newfoundland — many pages of speculation and argument have been, and will probably continue to be advanced in support of these various theories; and the reader who wishes to come to some definite conclusion on this vexed subject only rises from the study of these learned disquisitions with the feeling that a great mass of knowledge has been devoted to very little purpose except that purpose be to have the question still open, and give employment to learned antiquarians for all time to come

— J.G. Bourinot, Royal Society of Canada, 1891

The project to build a replica of John Cabot's Matthew *is a worthy commemoration of his great voyage of discovery in 1497... I hope that the "Bristol Cabot 500 Celebrations 1997" will both remind the people of Bristol of the city's great history and encourage them to emulate the spirit of their predecessors*

— *HRH Prince Philip, Duke of Edinburgh, Patron of the Matthew Project, Windsor Castle, 1992*

Such was the fascination with the Cabots and their voyages that by 1900 a Cabot bibliography listed 232 original references and another 579 secondary sources, published over four centuries in English, French, Spanish, Portuguese, and Latin. Since then, the Cabots have continued to exercise a mystique, made all the more remarkable because so little contemporary documentation about them has survived. Perhaps it is because the little that is known is so open to endless speculation that John Cabot's 1497 landfall has aroused such passionate controversy, often to the point of losing sight of his achievement.

A primary reason why the historical record is so sparse is that for the first half-century after John Cabot's voyages no mention of them appeared in any English histories, so forgotten had they become. Then, with Sebastian Cabot's 1547 return to England and the revival of interest in overseas ventures, English chroniclers of the day began publishing brief accounts of early voyages, but so lost in memory had become John Cabot that his voyages were attributed to Sebastian. It was recognized that whatever claim England had to North America, in the face of French and Portuguese claims, rested on the Cabot voyages. But not until the historian of early English exploration, Richard Hakluyt, reprinted in 1582 the letters patent granted by King Henry in 1496 did John Cabot begin to emerge from obscurity. Hakluyt made no attempt to reconcile the conflicting evidence over John and Sebastian and their voyages. Right into the nineteenth century, historians believed that only one voyage had taken place, and they remained utterly divided over the roles of Cabot father and son.

In 1831, there appeared anonymously and simultaneously in England and the United States a *Memoir of*

Opposite and top left: Prince Philip

Above: The Matthew *in the Avon River, Bristol*

Sebastian Cabot. The author's identity was well known. An eminent lawyer from Pittsburgh, Richard Biddle had resided in London for five years and had immersed himself in researching the history of the early discovery of America. As befits his profession, he took an adversarial approach, which, when combined with poorly arranged arguments, made his presentation often more confusing than enlightening. He attacked Richard Hakluyt with a vengeance, holding him primarily responsible for the confusion surrounding the Cabot voyages. Biddle reached the conclusion that John Cabot had never been more than a merchant and likely never went on any voyages. Sebastian was the great navigator to whom Henry VII had "yielded a ready ear to the bold theory and sanguine promises of the accomplished and enthusiastic young navigator." He argued that the first land seen by Sebastian had been neither Newfoundland nor Cape Breton, but Labrador. Although Biddle accused Hakluyt of writing his history of early discoveries for the glory of the English nation, which was unquestionably true, Biddle was equally anxious to claim the achievement of the first discovery of North America for the English race.

For all its obsession with Sebastian and dismissal of John, Biddle's work was the first serious critique of the available sources, and his research confirmed that there had been two voyages. Further confirmation came with the publication in 1864 of correspondence contemporary with the two voyages that had recently been found in the Venetian archives. Although the level of Cabot scholarship now rose dramatically, controversy increased all the more as Cabot's landfall became a question of intense debate.

After Biddle's death in 1847, the most serious student of Cabot scholarship was a Frenchman, Henry Harrisse, who studied law in the United States but then returned to France where he devoted his life to researching the Cabots. His cartographical researches led him initially to accept a Cape Breton landfall, but further investigation caused him to portray Sebastian as "an unmitigated charlatan" and to argue that John Cabot's 1497 landfall was Cape Chidley at the entrance to Hudson Bay. Another Cabot scholar and lawyer, William Deane, confined himself to calling Sebastian "the sphinx of American history for over three hundred years."

As the 400th anniversary of Cabot's 1497 voyage

approached, Canadians, inspired by race and English-Canadian nationalism, came to dominate the controversy. Annual meetings of the Royal Society of Canada became the forum for continuing debate. At the 1889 meeting, William Francis Ganong gave a paper on "Cartography to Champlain." At 25, and just then embarking on a brilliant scholarly career, he was a scion of the prominent St. Stephen's Ganongs and already had degrees from the University of New Brunswick and Harvard. (He was to receive his doctorate in botany from Munich University in 1894.) He brought a scientifically trained mind to a lifetime study of eastern Canadian cartography that remains unequalled in its depth, originality of deduction, and significance for early Canadian history. Ganong argued that the compiler of Sebastian's 1544 map may have used material from John Cabot's maps but also relied extensively on those of Jacques Cartier, who was Ganong's primary interest. He argued that, for his own reasons, Sebastian had placed *prima tierra vista* on Cape Breton Island: the map itself, however, was not, Ganong held, of a high standard for its day and was "unworthy" of Sebastian, or perhaps even a "forgery."

In 1891, the Right Reverend Michael Howley, Roman Catholic Bishop of St. John's, entered the fray as he informed readers of the *Magazine of American History*: "As a Newfoundlander, reared in the tradition which has been held from time immemorial, that 'Bonavista, happy light,' was the landfall, I feel loath to give it up without a struggle." The very name Cape Bonavista had long suggested to Newfoundlanders that it must have been John Cabot's landfall, and it was to have no more avid defender than Bishop Michael Howley.

In his 1497 letter to his Venetian brothers, Lorenzo Pasqualigo reported that Cabot had voyaged 700 leagues before sighting land, while in the first despatch to the Duke of Milan that unknown correspondent gave a figure of 400

Aspy Bay at the top of Cape Breton Island is believed by many to be John Cabot's 1497 landfall

leagues. This wide discrepancy led to much argument. Bishop Howley, however, flattered himself that he had "discovered the key to the mystery, and the means of reconciling all these conflicting testimonies." He argued that Cabot on his 1497 voyage had not turned west after reaching the Atlantic side of Ireland, but had continued northwards, as far as St. Kilda's or Rockall off Scotland. Here, he then turned west to reach Cape Farewell, Greenland — a distance of 400 leagues. Then, Cabot pushed on and first sighted land at Cape St. John near Bonavista — 300 leagues from Greenland, for a total Atlantic crossing of 700 leagues. Howley dismissed a Cape Breton landfall out of hand.

Two years later, in 1893, another Newfoundland cleric, the Reverend Moses Harvey, gave a paper entitled, "The Voyages and Discoveries of the Cabots" to the Nova Scotia Historical Society. Harvey's intellectual endeavours ranged from lectures on such topics as ancient Egypt and its monuments to writing a *Textbook of Newfoundland History* and contributing Newfoundland articles to the *Encyclopædia Britannica*. He had read extensively in the Cabot literature, so he spoke with confident knowledge of the most recent scholarship.

Harvey's presentation on Cabot, his arrival in England,

and his first voyage cannot be faulted for what was known in his day. He found slight evidence that the 1497 landfall could have been Bonavista, Bishop Howley's advocacy notwithstanding. Harvey concluded it must have been in Cape Breton, citing the 1544 map as the trustworthy "grand authority." In giving his lecture, Harvey had more on his mind than just another contribution to the Cabot debate. What really motivated him was his contention that if Columbus' great discovery had merited a celebration on the fourth centenary of his famous 1492 voyage, why should not Cabot be so honoured in 1897? Harvey credited Sebastian, not Columbus, with "undoubtedly" being the first to see continental America: the honour of being "the real discovers of North America" had to go to the Cabots. That North America was almost entirely occupied by an English-speaking population, with all its vast energies and accumulated wealth, had been "largely owing to the daring genius of the Cabots." Harvey proceeded to write the Secretary of the Royal Society of Canada proposing just such a celebration, setting in train the 1897 Cabot commemoration.

That Canadians were coming to possess the Cabots as vitally important to their history could not be better illustrated than by Samuel Edward Dawson. A native Haligonian, Dawson moved with his parents in 1847 to Montreal. In 1891 he became Queen's Printer to the Dominion Government. He had already received an honourary doctorate from Laval University and been elected a fellow of the Royal Society in recognition of his wide-ranging scholarship. His paper, "The Voyages of the Cabots in 1497 and 1498," given at the 1894 Royal Society meeting, proved to be the most extensive yet by a Canadian. His motivation clearly reflected emerging Canadian nationalism:

> *"For that part of continental America first trodden by Europeans is Canadian land, and to Canadians nothing concerning John Cabot can be considered foreign... Canadians should not quietly resign Cabot to other hands, for he is more to them than Columbus is to the people of the United States."*

After all, as he stressed, "solely upon the discoveries

Caboto primum reperta ("First found by Cabot"). "As a Newfoundlander," the learned judge claimed, "for Cape Bonavista the honour of being the first land seen in North America."

At the 1896 Royal Society meeting, Dawson chastised Prowse for taking such an uncritical approach, pointing out that, as there had been no settlement of Newfoundland until 1610, there could hardly be an "unbroken tradition" dating back to Cabot in 1497. He also noted that Harvey had accepted the Bonavista landfall, which had few advocates, and even James P. Howley, Director of Newfoundland's Geological Survey, held to a Labrador landfall. In a lecture delivered at Saint Patrick's Hall in St. John's, Bishop Howley responded to Dawson's idea of a Cape Breton landfall as "obviously absurd and impossible... to people born with a 'nautical sense,' as we here in Newfoundland."

In June 1897, the Royal Society gathered in Halifax, chosen because of all the controversies "as neutral ground on which all the disputants can happily meet without giving up their respective theories." In preparation for the honour bestowed on the city, *The Halifax Herald* had Harry Piers, the province's Assistant Legislative Librarian, write on Cabot. Piers' "The

of the Cabots have rested the original claims of the English race to a foothold upon this continent." Although he praised the labours of such scholars as Harrisse, he believed that Canadians could bring to the discussion the advantages of "an intimate knowledge which these learned men could not possess." He then proceeded to chastise Harrisse for his lack of geographical knowledge of the Canadian east coast. Dawson argued for a Cape Breton landing in 1497 and assumed that John Cabot died on the 1498 voyage, when the landfall had been Labrador.

Another Newfoundlander to enter the debate on Cabot's landfall was Judge Daniel Woodley Prowse. In his monumental *History of Newfoundland from the English, Colonial, and Foreign Records*, Prowse, like Bishop Howley, cited an unbroken tradition of Bonavista as the first land seen by Cabot. This was further confirmed by John Mason's Newfoundland map of around 1616, in which, opposite to Cape Bonavista, were the words *A*

Above: The John Cabot bust at Cape North, looking out into Aspy Bay. The Cape Breton Historical Society was responsible for having this monument placed. Its official unveiling took place on June 24th, 1959. A year earlier, on the same date, the Society unveiled a commemorative plaque to Cabot and the Matthew *voyage*

Opposite: A statue of John Cabot on the Bristol waterfront

*View of Cabot Tower,
St. John's*

Discovery of The Continent" was exceptionally well researched and his summary of Cabot's life and voyages cannot be faulted for its time. He traced the change in landfall theories and concluded Cape Breton now found the widest acceptance.

"In Honour of 'Good Old John Cabot'" was how the *Herald* entitled the June 24th proceedings at Nova Scotia's Province House for the unveiling of the Royal Society's commemorative plaque by the Governor-General, Lord Aberdeen. His Grace Cornelius O'Brien, Roman Catholic Archbishop of Halifax, presided, along with state and military representatives, two former mayors of Bristol, the Italian Consul-General, and, notably, a number of Mi'kmaq. Because 1897 also marked Queen Victoria's Diamond Jubilee, the plaque's wording noted that it was during her reign that "the Dominion of Canada extended from the shores first seen by Cabot four hundred years before, to the Pacific Coast." (Nova Scotia was then the country's most eastern province, so the wording could only refer to a Cape Breton landfall.)

Whatever the hopes the Royal Society had for dispassionate scholarly neutrality at Halifax, as its presiding President, Archbishop O'Brien would have none of it. Like his fellow cleric, Bishop Howley, O'Brien in his address that evening to the Society had no difficulty resolving all perplexing questions, harmonizing conflicting testimonies, and presenting as no longer "theory" but "settled fact" that Cabot's landfall was on Cape Breton Island.

When Judge Daniel Prowse read O'Brien's address, he gave vent to his fury in a letter to the Halifax *Morning Chronicle* that the paper entitled "The Claim of Newfoundland Stoutly Defended." Prowse set the tone of his diatribe in his opening lines: "Nova Scotians most deservedly enjoy the reputation of being amongst the shrewdest, most wide awake and humorous people in America. After reading this article they will be able to appreciate some of the absurdities connected with the

recent celebration proceedings in Halifax." A Cape Breton landing was "utterly untenable, opposed alike to common sense, reason and all the contemporary records." The learned and eloquent Archbishop had "let his Celtic imagination run riot." After one of the most confusing Cabot explications on record, the learned judge ended with as good a rhetorical flourish as can be found in all the Cabot literature:

The names Bonavista, oh! happy sight;
Bonaventura, oh! happy find, are just the

names the old explorer would give us coming
from his long tempest tossed voyage over
unknown seas, he first beheld the bold head-
land bright and green with the springing
verdure of June.

When it came to a Cabot memorial, Newfoundland, however, completely outdid Nova Scotia in 1897. Prowse was absolutely determined to have a suitable memorial erected to Cabot in St. John's, but he found no unanimity because many wanted instead a convalescent wing for the city's Victoria Hospital to commemorate Queen Victoria's Diamond Jubilee. But Prowse gained sufficient support within the mercantile community to have a signal tower built, while others went ahead with the convalescent wing. As June 1897 approached, Cabot fever swept Newfoundland. Although James Howley, the Director of the Newfoundland Geological Survey, offered to debate Prowse over a Labrador versus a Cape Bonavista landfall, for once Prowse refused to defend Bonavista. When the St. John's Mechanics' Institute held a billiards tourna- ment between sides representing Bonavista and Cape Breton, Bonavista won handily, and Bonavista appeared on a special commemorative stamp issued with the inscription "Cape Bonavista, the Landfall of Cabot."

With 22 June being Jubilee Day and the 24th Cabot Day, organizers decided to have the cornerstone cere- monies for both the signal tower, to be known as Cabot Tower, and the convalescent wing on the 22nd. A proto- col problem had to be resolved when Governor Sir Herbert Harley Murray refused to lay the tower's corner- stone because, as he informed the Colonial Secretary in

Bristol's Cabot Tower, erected as part
of the city's 1897 commemoration of
the 400th anniversary of the Matthew
voyage

London, it would be out of place to take part in a ceremony by "which Her Majesty's fame was to be celebrated in conjunction with that of a foreign adventurer."

Instead Bishop Howley, a far more appropriate choice, agreed to do the honour before an estimated crowd of 5,000. Cabot Tower began operation in June 1900 and continued to be used for signalling right down to 1958, for which mariners have Prowse to thank, as without him it would never have been built.

For their part, Bristol citizens had no problem celebrating a "foreign adventurer." They erected a memorial tower, and the Marquis of Dufferin laid its cornerstone on 24 June 1897. As a former Canadian Governor-General, he trod warily on the landfall question, confining himself to "on this very day the Cape of Bonavista, or whatever point on the coast of Newfoundland, Labrador, or Cape Breton the learned may determine." In a leader, *The Times* of London gave the honour to Cape Breton, while commenting that the "real achievement of John Cabot was that he showed

JOHN CABOT MAKES HIS LANDFALL / JEAN CABOT ABORDE LE PAYS

One of a series of stamps commemorating Canadian discovery issued in the 1980s

Englishmen... the path of empire."

As Cabot's quatercentenary celebrations passed into history and the century ended, two books appeared that did much to restore some balance to the Cabot debate. A Fellow of Merton College, Oxford, Charles Raymond Beazley, became the first academic historian to tackle the vexing questions surrounding the Cabot voyages. In his *John and Sebastian Cabot: The Discovery of North America*, he did so with a dispassionate evaluation of the surviving evidence. Beazley presented no theories and did not select one landfall over another. He was particularly effective in dealing with the "Sebastianized accounts" and gave full credit to John Cabot. Accurate translations of Cabot documents continued to pose difficulties, but with the 1911 publication of Henry Perceval Biggar's *The Precursors of Jacques Cartier*, scholars now had translations that have stood the test of time.

James Alexander Williamson's *The Voyages of the Cabots* proved to be the major work of the first half of the twentieth century. It included the most comprehensive presentation of documents and extracts from contemporary works yet published. Williamson brought his scholarship to bear most significantly in the placing of the Cabots, their documentation, and voyaging within the historical context of fifteenth- and sixteenth-century maritime discovery. In his "presumptive conclusions" on John Cabot's discoveries, Williamson suggested that for the 1497 voyage Cabot and the *Matthew* left Bristol on 2 May and returned on 6 August, having made a landfall near Cape Breton on 24 June, explored the Nova Scotian coast, and sighted a corner of Newfoundland. In 1498 he coasted as far as Delaware in search of Cathay before his crew perhaps forced him to return to Bristol, where he died shortly after. Williamson provided what evidence there was for a 1508 voyage by a young Sebastian as far north as Hudson Strait.

William Ganong received a copy of Williamson's work, a "sumptuous monograph" as he described it, just as a paper he gave at the 1929 meeting of the Royal Society was going to the press. Ganong put in an addendum titled "Voyages of John Cabot." What particularly interested him was Williamson's account of Sebastian's voyage of 1508. Ganong's paper was devoted to the Cabot voyages and the la Cosa map, and was the most detailed and exhaustive treatment of the map so far. He was indebted, as he readily admitted, to his years of correspondence dating from 1895 with G. R. F. Prowse, son of Judge Prowse. Although their exchanges on early maps reached voluminous proportions, they never met or addressed each other than very formally. The younger Prowse had begun researching early maps for his father's *History of Newfoundland*, and he devoted the remainder of his life to the subject. A recluse living most of his life in Manitoba and often in need of money, Prowse presented his findings in mimeographed form, which gave them a very limited circulation. An exception was a short paper, "The Cabot Landfall," printed in the proceedings of the Eighth International Geographic Congress at Washington in 1904. In it Prowse laid out his historical and cartographical arguments for a Bonavista landfall, which he was to uphold, some would say fanatically, until his death in 1946. Although he relied considerably on cartographical evidence, he gave also much weight to the "continuous Newfoundland tradition."

In 1955, the chance discovery of the John Day letter in the Spanish archives reopened the debate on the intractable question of Cabot's landfall. It also served as motivation for the Hakluyt Society and J. A. Williamson to publish in 1962, *The Cabot Voyages and Bristol Discovery under Henry VII, with the Cartography of the Voyages by R. A. Skelton*, a work unrivaled in Cabot scholarship. Williamson became the doyen of the Bristol School of Cabot historians, and to him the Day letter meant a southerly landfall for the 1497 voyage, perhaps as far south as Cape Sable or even Maine, while the cape from which Cabot sailed for England could have been on Cape Breton Island or at Cape Race.

The legendary Samuel Eliot Morison dismissed out of hand any idea of such southerly voyaging. In his widely read *The European Discovery of America*, he had little time for previous landfall theories. The Day letter provided the "precise navigational data, such as a master mariner like Columbus would want to know." Morison had Cabot take his latitude from Dursey Head and generally hold it until he first sighted either Cape Bauld or nearby Cape Dégrat.

A direct attack on Morison's Cape Bauld landfall came in 1973 not from any of the Bristol School, but from a very brief article in *The American Neptune* by Professor Jake Hubbard. He challenged Morison's theory that Cabot had coasted from Cape Bauld to Placentia Bay and back, 870 miles of extremely treacherous uncharted coastline, in just 26 days. Also, Morison had not taken into sufficient consideration Day's statement on the compass variation of 22 ½°, which Hubbard believed, in the wake of the storm cited by Day, would have caused Cabot to steer to a more southerly landfall at or near Bonavista.

Clearly, Day's "precise navigational data" had not resolved the landfall question, though almost all historians now agreed that Day's letter had become the primary source. However, it figured of far less importance in Fabian O'Dea's defence of a Bonavista landfall in the December's 1971 issue of the *Newfoundland Quarterly*. He argued that a Cape Breton landfall was untenable for navigational reasons, that la Cosa's map was useless for historical reconstruction, and dismissed Sebastian Cabot's 1544 map as evidence. For him, the navigational evidence, particularly the southward force of the Labrador Current and the compass variation cited in Day's letter, brought Cabot to first sight land off Bonavista.

O'Dea and Hubbard seem to be alone in more recent Cabot scholarship in holding out for Bonavista. David Quinn, for example, the English historian who succeeded Williamson as the doyen of the Bristol School with his *England and the Discovery of America, 1481-1620*, favours a landfall somewhere in Cape Breton, and a point of return at or near Cape Bauld. R. A. Skelton, for his *Dictionary of Canadian Biography* article on John Cabot, argues that the higher latitude is "irreconcilable" with the Day letter. Volume I of *The Historical Atlas of Canada*, on the other hand, follows Morison to northern Newfoundland. In *Canada Rediscovered*, Robert McGhee also adds his support to Morison's northern Newfoundland landfall. Allan Williams, however, in his *John Cabot and Newfoundland*, published by the Newfoundland Historical Society in 1996, follows Melvin Jackson, who in a 1963 article in the *Canadian Historical Review* argued for a Labrador landfall. Cabot would have then passed through the Strait of Belle Isle and coasted around to Cape Race before heading north to the Dursey Head latitude and home to Bristol.

The recently published *The Times Atlas of World Exploration*, perhaps in an attempt to be all things to all people, shows a Cape Breton landfall and has Cabot returning from Cape Bauld. Newfoundlanders can, however, take solace from a recent change of heart by *The Times* of London. In 1897, its leader writer had favoured Cape Breton as the landfall: his successor commented in a leader of 28 December 1996: "Like so much else [about Cabot], the exact spot [of his landfall] remains disputed: it could possibly have been Cape Breton Island, perhaps Labrador, but it was probably Newfoundland."

What all protagonists have to accept is that we lack evidence to reach a definite conclusion on Cabot's landfall. Only the most fortuitous finding of new evidence could change the fact that we will never know. Nor does it matter, for it is the voyage itself, and the European rediscovery of North America, that should merit our attention and upon which John Cabot's fame shall securely rest as a bold and expert mariner who crossed the Ocean Sea and found new land.

The 500th anniversary of Cabot's voyage in the *Matthew* offers Canadians, Newfoundlanders and Cape Bretoners alike, as well as the people of Bristol, the opportunity to celebrate as never before the man and his voyage of discovery. The Matthew Project has become the focus of the 1997 Cabot commemorative celebrations.

The idea to build in Bristol a replica of the *Matthew* was conceived in 1991. Plans went ahead: the HRH Prince Philip became Patron, it was decided to construct the replica at the historic Bristol docks, and Colin Mudie was engaged as naval architect. After extensive research (no plans of the first *Matthew* exist) he decided on a square-rigged caravel with an overall length of 73 feet, a beam of 19 feet 8 inches, and a draft of 7 feet. In the 1980s, Mudie had been involved in the research surrounding the raising of a Tudor ship, the *Mary Rose*, whose hull form he described as so sophisticated and beautiful that it was "streets ahead of what naval architects have been drawing for the past 100 years." His participation in that project proved of great assistance in designing a *Matthew* replica. The City of Bristol provided a historic and prominent site at Redcliffe Quay and an adjoining visitor centre. There, under a canopy, the *Matthew* took shape. Her construction required 26 oak trees for the hull, most of which came from trees blown down during a storm. Douglas fir was used for the decking, masts, and spars. Of her three masts, the tallest is 65 feet, and her sail area is 2,360 square feet of unbleached linen.

With much fanfare the *Matthew* was launched on 9 September 1995. During her sea trials under skipper David Alan-Williams, a member of the victorious New Zealand crew in the 1995 America's Cup, she went to London where the Canadian High Commissioner, Frederick Eaton, greeted her. Then on 2 May 1997 came the big moment, when, after a blessing by the Bishop of Bristol, the *Matthew* left Bristol for her seven-week voyage across the Atlantic. Bristol citizens turned out in large numbers to witness the departure and enjoy a giant party. On the other side of the Atlantic, around Newfoundland and in Cape Breton, a great welcome was being prepared for the *Matthew*. If John Cabot could once more sail the *Matthew* across the mysterious Ocean Sea, he would find that, after 500 years, his achievement is both well remembered and suitably commemorated.

BIBLIOGRAPHY

The writings on John Cabot are so extensive that this bibliographical note is confined to the most recent publications that are either still in print or should be readily available in libraries. For those interested in the earlier literature, George Winship Parker's *Cabot Bibliography*, published in 1900, is the pre-eminent source. There is a reprint of it in the Burt Franklin & Source Work Series, No. 99, 1967.

Although some contest his conclusions, James Williamson's *The Cabot Voyages and Bristol Discovery under Henry VII with The Cartography of the Voyages by R. A. Skelton* remains an indispensable reference. Williamson gathered together all the known original documents relating to Bristol voyaging before Cabot, Cabot's 1497 and 1498 voyages, and Sebastian's voyage to the northwest in 1508. These documents Williamson reproduced in translation and I have used them exclusively. He also provided an Introduction that for analysis of Cabot sources is unsurpassed in its exhaustiveness and balance. R. A. Skelton's *The Cartography of the Voyages* complements Williamson's Introduction and includes a list of references. Skelton is also the author of the *Dictionary of Canadian Biography* Articles on both John and Sebastian Cabot. For all that has been written on John Cabot, Skelton's biography remains the best summary we have of his life.

Historians in the second half of the twentieth century have done much to place the Cabot voyages in the context of early English and European maritime expansion. Aside from Williamson's work, that of David Quinn in his *England and the Discovery of America, 1481-1620* stands out, as does S. E. Morison's *The European Discovery of America*. In *The Westward Expansion*, edited by K. P. Andrews and others, Patrick McGrath's

"Bristol and America 1480-1631" reviews the evidence for pre-Cabot voyages from Bristol to the Grand Banks off Newfoundland and concludes that none likely took place. Still, the possibility of pre-Cabot voyages remains tantalizing, and those such as Robert McGhee in his *Canada Rediscovered* give credence to them. Similarly does Felipe Fernández-Armesto, as editor of *The Times Atlas of World Exploration*, a superb and monumental publication that will stand the test of time. Ian Wilson, a native of Bristol, in his popularly written *Columbus Myth*, builds his story around the theme of pre-Cabot and pre-Columbian discovery of America by Bristol seamen. He has Cabot reaching the mainland before Columbus.

I list below those works that are in my opinion the most useful of recent additions to the continuing volume of Cabot literature:

Andrews, K. R., N. P. Canny and P. E. H. Hair, eds. *The Westward Enterprise: English activities in Ireland, the Atlantic, and America 1480-1650* (Liverpool: Liverpool University Press, 1978).

Candow, James, "Daniel Woodley Prowse and the Origin of the Cabot Tower," *Research Bulletin No. 155*, June 1981, Parks Canada.

Davies, Arthur, "The 'English Coasts' on the Map of Juan de la Cosa," *Imago Mundi*, Vol. 13, 1956, pp. 26-29.

Fergusson, C. Bruce, "Cabot's Landfall," unpublished paper in the Fergusson Papers, Box 1846, F5/36, Public Archives of Nova Scotia.

Fernández-Armesto, Felipe, *The Times Atlas of World Exploration* (London: Times Books, a division of HarperCollins Publishers, 1991).

Firstbrook, Peter, *The Voyage of the Matthew: John Cabot and the Discovery of North America* (BBC Books, published in Canada by McCelland & Stewart Inc., Toronto, 1997)

Fuson, Robert H., "The John Cabot Mystique," in Stanley R. Lamer and Dennis Reinhartz, *Essays on the History of North American Discovery and Exploration*, Arlington Texas: A&M University Press, 1988.

Ganong, F. W., *Crucial Maps in the Early Cartography and Place-Nomenclature of the Atlantic Coast of Canada*, with Introduction, Commentary, and Map Notes by Theodore E. Layng (Toronto: University of Toronto Press, in cooperation with the Royal Society of Canada, 1964).

Hoffman, Bernard, G., *Cabot to Cartier: Sources for a Historical Ethnography of Northeastern North America, 1497-1550* (Toronto, 1961).

Hubbard, Jake T. W., "John Cabot's Landfall: Cape Dégrat or Cape Bonavista?" *The American Neptune* (July 1973), pp. 174-77.

Jackson, Melvin H., "The Labrador Landfall of John Cabot: The 1497 Voyage Reconsidered," *Canadian Historical Review*, XLIV (1963).

Juricek, John T., "John Cabot's First Voyage," *Smithsonian Journal of History,* II (1967-8), 1-22.

Layng, Theodore E, *Sixteenth-Century Maps Relating to Canada* (Ottawa: Public Archives of Canada, 1956).

McGhee, Robert, *Canada Rediscovered* (Canadian Museum of Civilization, 1991).

Morison, Samuel Eliot, *The European Discovery of America: The Northern Voyages A. D.500-1600* (New York: Oxford University Press, 1971).

O'Dea, Fabian, "Cabot's landfall —Yet Again," Lecture to the Newfoundland Historical Society. St. John's, 1971, *Newfoundland Quarterly*, Vol. 4, No. 2 (December 1971), pp. 15-24.

Phillips, William D. and Carla Rahn Phillips, *The World of Christopher Columbus* (Cambridge: Cambridge University Press, 1992).

Quinn, David., *North America from Earliest Discovery to First Settlements: The Norse Voyages to 1612* (New York: Harper & Row, 1977).

Quinn, David, *England and the Discovery of America, 1481-1620* (New York: Alfred A. Knopf, 1974).

Ruddock, Alwyn A., "John Day of Bristol and the English Voyages across the Atlantic before 1497," *Geographical Journal*, 132, 1966, pp. 225-33.

Skelton, R. A., "John Cabot," *Dictionary of Canadian Biography*, Vol. 1.

True, David O., "Cabot Explorations in North America," reprint from *Imago Mundi: A Review of Early Cartography,* edited by Leo Bagrow, 1956, Stockholm.

Vigneras, L. A., "New Light on the 1497 Cabot Voyage to America," *Hispanic American Historical Review*, Vol. 36 (1956), pp. 503-09.

Vigneras, L. A., "The Cape Breton Landfall: 1494 or 1497," *Canadian Historical Review*, Vol. 38 (1957), pp. 219-28.

Williams, Alan F., *John Cabot and Newfoundland* (St. John's: Newfoundland Historical Society, 1996).

Williamson, James A., *The Cabot Voyages and Bristol Discovery Under Henry VII with The Cartography of the Voyages by R. A. Skelton,* The Hakluyt Society, 2nd Series, No. CXX (Cambridge: Cambridge University Press, 1962).

Wilson, Ian, *John Cabot and the Matthew* (S. John's: Breakwater, 1996)

Wilson, Ian., *The Columbus Myth: Did Men of Bristol Reach America before Columbus?* (London: Simon & Schuster, 1991).

INDEX

PHOTO CREDITS

Top=T, Bottom=B, Right=R, Left=L

Accademia, Venice/e.t. archive: p. 16. Accademia, Venice/Cameraphoto/Art Resource NY: p. 14. Accademia, Venice/Scala/Art Resource NY: p. 11. Beaton Institute, University College of Cape Breton, photograph by Paul Prendergast: p. 63. Bibliothèque Nationale: p. 56. Birgitta Wallace Collection, Parks Canada: p. 26, C.C. Rafn, Antiquitates Americanae; p. 31, 33. Bristol Record Office: p. 29, 30. *Bristol Evening Post* (U.K.)/Godrevy Publications' *Matthew* by Steve Martin & Colin Sanger: p. 5. Bristol Tourism: p. 34, 62, 65. British Library: p. 21, 22. British Library/Bridgeman Art Gallery: p. 28, 37, 49. Canada Post Corporation/National Archives of Canada: p. 7TL, POS-001559; 40, POS-001759; 43 TR, POS-00336; 51, POS-001553; 66, POS-002520. City of Bristol Museum and Art Gallery: p. 32. City of Bristol Museum and Art Gallery/Bridgeman Art Library: p. 38. Civitates Orbis Terrarum: p. 12, 19, 47. Colin Sanger/Morek Cards: front cover, p. 1. Correr Museum,Venice/e.t. archive: p. 15B. e.t. archive: p. 35. Godrevy Publications' *Matthew* by Steve Martin & Colin Sanger: p. 6. Lewis Parker, courtesy of the University College of Cape Breton Art Gallery: p. 45. Marciana, Venice/e.t. archive: p. 17. Martin Chainey, Bristol: p. 2, 58, 59 TL & BR. Max (U.K.)/Godrevy Publications' *Matthew* by Steve Martin & Colin Sanger: p. 4. Musée Stewart: p. 3, 42, 43 TL, 48. Museo Naval, Madrid/Heritage Research Associates: p. 55. Naval Museum Genoa/e.t. archive: cover; p. 8, 10, 25. Newfoundland Historical Society: p. 41; backcover. Pamela Coristine/photograph by Bob Hong: p. 64. Private Collection, Courtesy of Philip Mould/Bridgeman Art Gallery: p. 36TL. Provost and Fellows of Eton College, Windsor/Bridgeman Art Library: p. 15T. Royal Chapel Granada, Spain/e.t. archive: p. 24. Topkapu Museum, Istanbul/e.t. archive: p. 18. Tourism Nova Scotia: p. 7 BL, 46, 60. Uffizi Gallery, Florence/e.t. archive: p. 36TR.